ISRAEL
Chosen By God

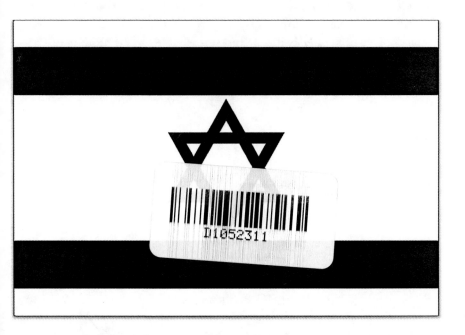

DAVID HOCKING

HFT publications

ISRAEL: Chosen by God

by David Hocking

ISBN: 978-0-9828563-1-4 Paperback

Published by:

HFT Publications
P.O. Box 3927
Tustin, CA 92781
1-800-75-BIBLE

NOTE: Unless noted otherwise, all Scripture is taken from the Holy Bible, King James Version.

TABLE OF CONTENTS

Part I
THE EXISTENCE OF ISRAEL

Part II
THE HISTORY OF ISRAEL

ISRAEL: Chosen by God

Part III
THE PROPHECIES ABOUT ISRAEL

PREFACE

No nation or people in human history have experienced what Israel has. Born and begun by a direct revelation from God; destroyed and scattered by military invasions; persecuted, hated, and murdered for no other reason than being what they are — the people of God! Some call it a "modern miracle" — Israel arises out of the dust and takes its place among the nations of the world once again, only to discover that the hatred and hostilities of the past have never gone away, and its right to exist questioned once more.

Israel faces today an unparalleled attempt by other nations to deny its right to exist, and to remove it from its land and its place in history. But, Israel has not gone away — it is still here! Even the attempts of Christians (who should know better!) to replace Israel's existence with its own concepts of the "church" (sometimes called "replacement theology") have failed to diminish what appears to be the continual fulfillment of ancient Bible prophecies.

ISRAEL: Chosen by God

This book is a sincere effort to describe and establish what the Bible actually says about this nation, land, and people we call "Israel."

No apologies will be made for drawing conclusions that are based on biblical mandates. Israel has no right to exist apart from a Divine plan and purpose. The thesis of this book is that Israel is the "centerpiece" of God's plan for human history. Israel has been "chosen by God" and no attempts by the creatures He has made will ever thwart or change His Divine purpose.

INTRODUCTION

Many excellent books have been written about Israel, and in one sense, we don't need another one! However, a simple presentation of Biblical facts about the existence, history, and prophecies concerning Israel seems more needed today with all the turmoil and political unrest concerning Israel's right to the Land, the threats to its survival and plans of terrorists to destroy her.

Added to the above are the confusion and controversies developing within Christian churches over the place of Israel in God's prophetic program. This confusion centers in the teaching of what has been called "Replacement Theology."

Simply put, "Replacement Theology" is the belief that the Church has replaced Israel in God's prophetic program for the future.

Those who hold to this belief base their understanding on the justice and judgment of God. They believe that Israel's sin and disobedience was judged by God and His eternal covenant with them was cancelled.

Most believe that this fact occurred in 70 AD with the Roman invasion and the destruction of Jerusalem and the Second Temple (restored by Herod the Great). Throughout this book we will make reference to this growing debate and the effect it is having upon the Nation of Israel today.

It is important to distinguish between the following words and to understand their biblical and historical differences:

✦ JEW — *ethnicity*

✦ JEWISH — *practice*

✦ HEBREW — *language*

✦ JUDAISM — *religion*

Judaism, the religion of Jewish people, expresses itself through many unique beliefs and practices.

For example:

✦ ULTRA-ORTHODOX

✦ ORTHODOX

✦ REFORMED

✦ CONSERVATIVE

✦ MESSIANIC

Within these traditional settings, there are many variations and differences. The last category is the most controversial. Most Jewish groups believe that if a Jewish person comes to believe that a given person in history is the Messiah (especially — Yeshua) then that person is no longer Jewish.

This is indeed strange in that one of the 13 principles of the great Rabbi Maimonides is a personal belief in a personal Messiah.

Many Jews believe that the so-called "Messianic Jewish Congregations" are nothing more than Gentile Christians trying to "play Jew." Unfortunately, this is often the case. Many of these congregations have more Gentiles attending than Jews.

However, in all fairness, it is utterly ridiculous to say that a Jewish person who believes that Yeshua ben Yoseph (Jewish teacher who claimed to be the Messiah — first century AD) is the true Messiah is therefore no longer a Jew.

The immigration and aliyah problems of Israel give clear evidence that deciding who is a Jew and who is not a Jew is no longer an easy matter to settle.

Is the issue physical descent or religious beliefs? Or both?

In addition to the above questions, we have the problems of inter-marriage (Jew and Gentile) and the desire to assimilate into the culture and customs of the place where a Jewish person might choose to live.

If a given person claims to be Jewish, but has only a Jewish father, but a Gentile mother, is that child "Jewish"? Israel today seems to require not only evidence of a Jewish mother, but also a maternal grandmother. But, in the Bible, the Jewish descent seems clearly traced through the man, not the woman.

While we must inevitably "touch" on these issues, the purpose of this book is to give a brief Biblical and historical understanding. There are many volumes that discuss in detail the problems presented in the preceding paragraphs.

If you desire a simple and clear understanding about the existence, history, and prophecies of the Nation of Israel — then this book is for you! It is not an attempt to be exhaustive on any of its subjects and discussions.

Our sincere desire is to give a volume that is easy to understand and one that is rooted in Biblical teachings and understanding.

May the LORD GOD of Israel encourage all of us to base what we believe upon the truths of the Bible, and not human opinion!

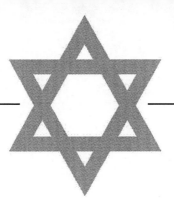

Part I

THE EXISTENCE OF ISRAEL

"And I will plant them upon their land, and they shall no more be pulled up out of their land which I have given them, saith the LORD thy God."

Amos 9:15

Chapter 1
THE BEGINNING

Where did Israel come from? How did it come to exist among the nations of the world?

The first usage of the name "Israel" is found in Genesis 32:28 when Jacob "wrestled" with a "man" all night long. Jacob's name was changed to "Israel."

"Thy name shall be called no more Jacob, but Israel: for as a prince hast thou power with God and with men, and hast prevailed."

Some say that the name "Israel" refers to the Hebrew word *sar* which means *"prince."* Others believe it is connected to a word meaning "wrestling." Therefore, the name means "prince of God" or "wrestling with God." The story in Genesis 32 could be emphasized either way. The hollow of Jacob's thigh was touched and became *"out of joint"* — it shrank!

The term *"the children of Israel"* is not found in the Bible until Genesis 49:28 where we read of the prophecies of

Jacob about his 12 sons and then these words: *"All these are the twelve tribes of Israel."*

There is no mention of the name "Israel" after the global deluge that destroyed the planet and its population.

In Isaiah 43:1 we read: *"But now thus saith the LORD that created thee, O Jacob, and He that formed thee, O Israel."* It is fascinating to read the Hebrew text of this verse and realize that the word translated *"created"* is the Hebrew word *"bara"* which appears in the very first verse of the Bible — *"In the beginning God created…"*

In other words, Israel was *"created"* by God and was not simply a "genetic result."

It is true that Israel came by physical descent from the son of Noah named *"Shem"* which is the Hebrew word for "name." The descendants of Shem are listed in Genesis 10:21-31. Shem had five sons, one of whom was named "Arphaxad." His descendants bring us to Terah, the father of Abram (Genesis 11:27), whose name was changed to "Abraham" (Genesis 17:5-8).

It is impossible to understand the "beginning" of Israel apart from Abraham. It was to Abraham (Genesis 12:1-3) that God gave His everlasting and unconditional covenant, and repeated it to his son Isaac (Genesis 26:3), and to his grandson, Jacob (Genesis 35:9-12). These three are known as the "fathers" of Israel.

The Bible makes a huge case of one simple fact — Abraham "believed God."

Chapter 2
THE COVENANT

The first "covenant" that God gave to humanity was the promise He made to Noah immediately after the worldwide flood. In Genesis 9:8-17 we learn that God promised that He would never again destroy the earth with a global flood. The rainbow in the sky was the sign of that covenant.

But, the covenant that dominates much of the Bible is the one God gave to Abraham in Genesis 12:1-3:

> *"Now the LORD had said unto Abram, Get thee out of thy country, and from thy kindred, and from thy father's house, unto a land that I will shew thee: And I will make of thee a great nation, and I will bless thee, and make thy name great; and thou shalt be a blessing: And I will bless them that bless thee, and curse him that curseth thee; and in thee shall all families of the earth be blessed."*

The first promise was *"a land that I will shew thee."*
The second promise was *"a great nation"* and the third
promise — *"in thee shall all families of the earth be blessed."*

+ LAND

+ NATION

+ DESCENDANT

Racially, there are only two groups in the world: Jews
and Gentiles. The word *"families"* is the Hebrew word
goyim and is translated as "nations, peoples, families,
heathen, and Gentiles." All nations will be blessed through
a coming descendant of Abraham — it is referring to the
MESSIAH, the promised Seed of Abraham!

The sign of this strategic covenant was and is circumcision of all male babies on the 8th day of their lives
(Genesis 17:9-14). Those who did not obey the sign of
the covenant were *"cut off"* from the provisions of this
covenant.

FOUR IMPORTANT FACTS ABOUT GOD'S COVENANT TO ABRAHAM

Unusual

A covenant is usually made between two parties and
is dependent upon each performing the details of that
covenant.

God's covenant to Abraham, Isaac, and Jacob is quite "unusual" because it is based on the immutability of God Himself, and NOT on the performance of humanity!

Hebrews 6:13-18 makes this very clear. God's promise to Abraham was based on two immutable (unchangeable) things: One is God's own character — He NEVER changes (Malachi 3:6)! Secondly, it is based on God's oath — He could swear by no one greater, and *"it was impossible for God to lie."*

Unique

This covenant of God to Abraham is also quite unique when compared with the covenants, treaties, and promises of man.

God's covenant is "unique" because it depends solely upon God's faithfulness, not human merit or worth!

Psalm 89:30-34 says: *"If his children forsake My law, and walk not in My judgments; If they break My statutes, and keep not My commandments; Then will I visit their transgression with the rod, and their iniquity with stripes. Nevertheless My lovingkindness will I not utterly take from him, nor suffer My faithfulness to fail. My covenant will I not break, not alter the thing that is gone out of My lips."*

God's faithfulness was promised by God in the beginning of Israel's history!

Deuteronomy 7:9 says: *"Know therefore that the LORD thy God, He is God, the faithful God..."* God did not choose Israel because they were greater in number or ability; His choice was based on His love and faithfulness. The world would know what kind of a God He is by how He would be faithful to His people, Israel, even when they were unfaithful to Him.

Unending

When we read that this covenant is everlasting, that means it can never be broken or changed. It is not dependent upon the circumstances of human life and history. No events can ever cancel or change this covenant.

Long after the giving of this everlasting covenant to Abraham, Isaac, and Jacob, we read these words in Psalm 105:8-11: *"He hath remembered His covenant forever, the word which He commanded to a thousand generations. Which covenant He made with Abraham, and His oath unto Isaac; and confirmed the same unto Jacob for a law, and to Israel for an EVERLASTING covenant: saying, Unto thee will I give the land of Canaan, the lot of your inheritance."*

FACTS:

1. The covenant was given to Abraham 4,000 years ago.

2. The Psalms of David (quoted above) were written over 3,000 years ago! One thousand years after

the covenant was given, God confirmed that it was still in force.

Unconditional

This wonderful covenant and promise of God is not based on human deeds and achievements. It is based on faith in the God Who promised it. The New Testament lays out this argument in Romans 4:

> *"What shall we say then that Abraham our father, as pertaining to the flesh, hath found? For if Abraham were justified by works, he hath whereof to glory; but not before God. For what saith the scripture? Abraham believed God, and it was counted unto him for righteousness."*

Abraham simply believed what God had promised to him. Faith is the necessary requirement, but whether we believe it or not, it is still true!

Our works do not put God's covenant into force! This unconditional covenant requires faith in what God has already promised and what He Himself will perform! He will keep His Word!

Chapter 3
THE FATHERS

When Jewish people speak of "the Fathers" they are referring to Abraham, Isaac, and Jacob.

Exodus 3:15-16

"And God said moreover unto Moses, Thus shalt thou say unto the children of Israel, The LORD of your Fathers, the God of Abraham, the God of Isaac, and the God of Jacob, hath sent me unto you: this is My Name forever, and this is My memorial unto all generations. Go, and gather all the elders of Israel together, and say unto them, The LORD God of your FATHERS, the God of Abraham, of Isaac, and of Jacob, appeared unto me, saying, I have surely visited you, and seen that which is done to you in Egypt."

Exodus 4:5

"That they may believe that the LORD God of their

FATHERS, the God of Abraham, the God of Isaac, and the God of Jacob, hath appeared unto thee."

Deuteronomy 1:8

"Behold, I have set the land before you; go in and possess the land which the LORD sware unto your FATHERS, Abraham, Isaac, and Jacob, to give unto them to their seed after them."

It is clear from the above verses that the covenant involved the "land" which the LORD promises to the "fathers" and "to their seed after them." Therefore, it is correct to say that the "land" was given to the physical descendants of Abraham, Isaac, and Jacob!

Deuteronomy 4:31

"For the LORD thy God is a merciful God; He will not forsake thee, neither destroy thee, nor forget the covenant of thy FATHERS which He sware unto them."

Deuteronomy 4:37-38

"And because He loved thy FATHERS, therefore He chose their seed after them, and brought thee out in His sight with His mighty power out of Egypt; to drive out nations from before thee greater and mightier than thou art, to bring thee in, to give thee their land for an inheritance, as it is this day."

Over 400 years after Israel went into bondage in Egypt, the LORD God made it very clear that His goal was to give the physical descendants of Abraham, Isaac, and Jacob, the land that He had promised to their "fathers."

> Deuteronomy 6:10
>
> *"And it shall be, when the LORD thy God shall have brought thee into the land which He sware unto thy FATHERS, to Abraham, to Isaac, and to Jacob...."*

The Bible makes it clear that God gave the land to the "fathers" and their physical descendants. To emphasize that fact the Bible uses this phrase repeatedly *"which He sware unto thy FATHERS..."* It was based on the oath of God Himself, and He could swear by none greater than Himself! (cf. Deuteronomy 6:10, 18, 23; 7:8, 12, 13; 8:1, 18; 9:5; 10:11; 11:9, 21)

> Deuteronomy 26:15
>
> *"Look down from Thy holy habitation, from heaven, and bless Thy people Israel, and the land which Thou hast given us, as Thou swarest unto our FATHERS, a land that floweth with milk and honey."*

> Deuteronomy 30:20
>
> *"that thou mayest dwell in the land which the*

ISRAEL: Chosen by God

LORD *sware unto thy* FATHERS, *to Abraham, to Isaac, and to Jacob, to give them."*

Yes, the land belongs to the "FATHERS" (Abraham, Isaac, and Jacob) and their descendants!

Chapter 4
CHOSEN BY GOD

Many people do not believe or accept the Bible's teaching that Israel was and is "CHOSEN BY GOD." Their beliefs and opinions do not change God's declarations about His people. The Bible is clear — God chose Israel!

People say "they do not deserve it" for all that they have done! That is true! But God's promises to them are NOT based on whether they deserve it or not. None of us deserve to be "chosen by God."

Deuteronomy 7:6 says, *"For thou art an holy people unto the LORD thy God: the LORD thy God hath chosen thee to be a special people unto Himself, above all people that are upon the face of the earth."* Verse 7 continues: *"The LORD did not set His love upon you, nor choose you, because ye were more in number than any people; for ye were the fewest of all people."*

Deuteronomy 14:2 repeats the great truth that God has chosen Israel as His own people: *"For thou art an holy* people unto the LORD thy God, and the LORD hath chosen thee to be a peculiar people unto Himself, above all nations that are upon the earth."

Notice the following about God's choice:

1. HOLY (means "separate")

2. PECULIAR (unique)

3. UNTO HIMSELF (God's choice is for Himself!)

4. ABOVE ALL NATIONS (Israel is the most important nation in the history of the world!)

I Chronicles 16:13

"O ye seed of Israel His servant, ye children of Jacob, His chosen ones."

Psalm 33:12

"Blessed is the nation whose God is the LORD; and the people whom He hath chosen for His own inheritance."

Psalm 135:4

"For the LORD hath chosen Jacob unto Himself, and Israel for His peculiar treasure."

Isaiah 41:8-9

"But thou, Israel, art My servant, Jacob whom I have chosen, the seed of Abraham, My friend.

Thou whom I have taken from the ends of the earth, and called thee from the chief men thereof, and said unto thee, Thou art My servant; I have chosen thee, and not cast thee away."

Isaiah 44:1-2

"Yet now hear, O Jacob My servant; and Israel, whom I have chosen: Thus saith the LORD that made thee, and formed thee from the womb, which will help thee; Fear not, O Jacob, My servant; and thou, Jesurun, whom I have chosen."

There is no doubt about it — Israel was and is "CHOSEN OF GOD."

This fact is based solely upon God's sovereign choice, not Israel's merit or worthiness. It was and is grace alone that is behind the choice of God.

All true believers in the Messiah of Israel, Jew and Gentile, are said to be "chosen" by God. Ephesians 1:4 says: *"According as He hath chosen us in Him before the foundation of the world…"*

One of the amazing passages of the Bible about the choice of God is found in I Corinthians 1:27-29: *"But God hath chosen the foolish things of the world to confound the wise; and God hath chosen the weak things of the world to confound the things which are mighty; and base things of the world, and things which are despised, hath God chosen, yea,* and things which are not, to bring to nought things that are: That no flesh should glory in His presence."

Notice the Bible's description of the believers who are "chosen" of God:

✦ FOOLISH

✦ WEAK

✦ BASE

✦ DESPISED

But, God's choice is NOT dependent on human ability, talent, or personality traits; The Bible is clear — "no flesh should glory in His presence."

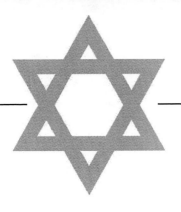

Part II

THE HISTORY OF ISRAEL

"Now all these things happened unto them for examples: and they are written for our admonition, upon whom the ends of the world are come."

I Corinthians 10:11

Chapter 5
ISAAC AND ISHMAEL

The history of Israel begins with God's revelation to Abraham. He promised Him three things:

✦ LAND

✦ NATION

✦ DESCENDANT

Abraham's wife, Sarah, was barren and Abraham would naturally be quite concerned as to how God would fulfill His promises to him when he and his wife were not able to have children.

Romans 4:17-22 is a remarkable commentary on Abraham's situation and his confidence in the promises and covenant of God:

"As it is written, I have made thee a father of many nations, before Him whom he believed, even God, Who quickeneth the dead, and calleth those things which be not as though they were. Who against hope, believed in hope, that he might become the

father of many nations; according to that which was spoken, So shall thy seed be. And being not weak in faith, he considered not his own body now dead, when he was about an hundred years old, neither yet the deadness of Sarah's womb: He staggered not at the promise of God through unbelief; but was strong in faith, giving glory to God; And being fully persuaded that, what He had promised, He was able also to perform, and therefore it was imputed to him for righteousness."

According to the account in Genesis 12:4 Abraham was 75 years old when he came to the Land of Canaan. Because Sarah was barren — unable to have any children, she suggested to Abraham that he attempt to have children by their Egyptian handmaid named Hagar. The plan worked. Hagar conceived and she bore Ishmael to Abraham.

Genesis 16:3 indicates that Abraham was now 85 years old.

But Sarah soon realized she had made a mistake. Tension between her and Hagar caused the handmaid to leave with her new baby. The Angel of the LORD found her out in the wilderness and told her to return to Sarah and submit to her. The Angel also said these words to her (Genesis 16:10): *"I will multiply thy seed exceedingly, that it shall not be numbered for multitude."* The Angel also told Hagar to name the boy "Ishmael" —

"because the LORD hath heard thy affliction."

According to Genesis 16:12 Ishmael will be *"a wild man; his hand will be against every man, and every man's hand against him; and he shall dwell in the presence of all his brethren."*

Genesis 16:16 records that Abraham was 86 years old when Ishmael was born.

Genesis 17:20 says this about Ishmael: *"And as for Ishmael, I have heard thee: Behold, I have blessed him, and will make him fruitful, and will multiply him exceedingly; twelve princes shall he beget, and I will make him a great nation."*

However, the LORD made it clear to Abraham that His covenant would be established with Isaac.

Because circumcision was the sign of God's covenant with Abraham, he, at age 99 years, along with his son, Ishmael, at age 13, was circumcised (Genesis 17:24-25).

The miraculous birth of Isaac occurred exactly as the LORD had predicted it would. Abraham was 100 years old, and Sarah was 90. Isaac was circumcised on the 8th day of his life.

But, as the boys got older, things were not good between them, and Hagar and Ishmael had to leave.

Sarah died at age 127 years (Genesis 23:1) and Abraham took another wife, Keturah (Genesis 25:1-3), who bore him six sons. Abraham died at age 175 (Genesis 25:7).

Isaac and Ishmael buried Abraham in the Cave of Machpelah in Hebron, which Abraham bought as a burial place for Sarah.

Ishmael died at age 137 (Genesis 25:17) and had 12 sons, that we recognize today as the "fathers" of the Arab peoples of the Middle East. Although many people in the Middle East are not Arab in descent, it was a son of Ishmael's second son, Kedar, who became the leader of Islam, and established Arabic as the language of the Muslims.

Interestingly, in the religion of Islam, its followers believe that Abraham took Ishmael, NOT Isaac, up to Mount Moriah, the story recorded in Genesis 22.

Muslims believe that the Jews changed the original text from Ishmael to Isaac, but there is no historical evidence to prove their point, and no Hebrew text of Genesis 22 ever read "Ishmael."

The problem of history is that people do not read and study the Bible (the most accurate and reliable account of ancient history), but rather make up their own minds as to what happened. The problem today is often stated to be between Jew and Arab. But, it is really between Israel and Islam! Over 50% of the Arabs profess to be Christian in background and belief. Many of the so-called "Arab" countries of the Middle East are NOT Arab at all in terms of physical descent. Many Arabs live within those countries. They would include Iran, Iraq, Jordan, Egypt, and even

Saudi Arabia — they are not "Arabs" even though people today try to argue that they are.

In trying to understand the historical background of the Nation of Israel, we have the following Biblical facts:

ISHMAEL

(father of 12 sons — Arabs)

Nebajoth	Kedar	Adbeel
Mibsam	Mishma	Dumah
Massa	Hadar	Tema
Jetur	Naphish	Kedemah

(found in Genesis 25:13-16)

ISAAC

(father of two sons)

Jacob   Esau

(found in Genesis 25:19-26)

Chapter 6
JACOB AND ESAU

The Bible is clear that God's covenant with Abraham was to be established with his son, Isaac, NOT with Ishmael. God promised to bless the descendants of Ishmael and make them a *"great nation."*

That brings us to the problem of Isaac and Rebekah's two sons, Jacob and Esau.

Often in Christian literature we read a negative report on the life of Jacob. He symbolizes the worst in character — a deceiving, conniving, manipulative man who did great harm to his brother, Esau.

But, the Bible presents an entirely different picture of Jacob. In Malachi 1:2-3a we read: *"I have loved you, saith the LORD. Yet ye say, Wherein hast Thou loved us? Was not Esau Jacob's brother? saith the LORD; yet I loved Jacob.*

"And I hated Esau..." This Old Testament background is behind a fascinating commentary in the New Testament Book of Romans, chapter 9. In verses 10-16 it says:

> "And not only this; but when Rebecca also had conceived by one, even by our father Isaac; (For the children being not yet born, neither having done any good or evil, that the purpose of God according to election (choice) might stand, not of works, but of Him that calleth;) It was said unto her, The elder shall serve the younger. As it is written, Jacob have I loved, but Esau have I hated. What shall we say then? Is there unrighteousness with God? God forbid. For He saith to Moses, I will have mercy on whom I will have mercy, and I will have compassion on whom I will have compassion. So then it is not of him that willeth, nor of him that runneth, but of God that sheweth mercy."

We also have a commentary in the Book of Hebrews about Esau. In Hebrews 12:15-17:

> "Looking diligently lest any man fail of the grace of God; lest any root of bitterness springing up trouble you, and thereby many be defiled; Lest there be any fornicator, or profane person, as Esau, who for one morsel of meat sold his birthright. For ye know how that afterward, when he would have inherited the blessing, he was rejected: for he found no place of repentance, though he sought it carefully with tears."

Putting these passages together, we come up with a completely different picture than is often presented by a few Bible teachers.

God had a special love for Jacob, and the Bible says He *"hated Esau."* Most of us are not comfortable with these words.

Yet, in Psalm 5:5 we read that God *"hatest all workers of iniquity."*

Esau is the ancestor of Edom, which is found today in the territory south of Amman, Jordan.

Rebekah is the one who received a direct revelation from God about the twins to be born in her womb. Genesis 25:23 says: *"And the LORD said unto her, Two nations are in thy womb, and two manner of people shall be separated from thy bowels; and the one people shall be stronger than the other people; and the elder shall serve the younger."*

But, because Isaac had a special love for Esau, he wanted him to receive the blessing of the firstborn. Rebekah knew that this was NOT the will of God. In urging her son, Jacob, to make his father believe he was Esau, was a matter of obedience to the known revealed will of God. It was Isaac who was not obeying the direct revelation of the LORD to Rebekah. Jacob became afraid of Esau.

Genesis 25:34 tells us that *"Esau despised his birthright."*

Esau lost both his birthright and the blessing of the firstborn. We read his words in Genesis 27:36: *"Is not he rightly named Jacob? For he hath supplanted me these two times: he took away my birthright; and behold, now he hath taken away my blessing."*

With many tears, Esau begged his father Isaac to bless him. Isaac answered with these words (Genesis 27:39-40) *"Behold, thy dwelling shall be the fatness of the earth, and of the dew of heaven from above; and by thy sword shalt thou live, and shalt serve thy brother; and it shall come to pass when thou shalt have the dominion, that thou shalt break his yoke from off thy neck."*

To this blessing of Esau we read in verse 41: *"And Esau hated Jacob because of the blessing wherewith his father blessed him."*

Esau made plans to kill Jacob in the future, and that ancient animosity remains until this day. Esau married two women who were Hittites. They were a *"grief of mind unto Isaac and to Rebekah* (Genesis 26:35)." Isaac then urged Jacob to get a wife from their family in Padanaram, not a wife of the daughters of Canaan.

In Genesis 33 we learn of the meeting between Jacob and Esau. The result was a measure of peace. Esau returned to the mountains of Seir, and Jacob went to Succoth and built a house there.

Chapter 6: Jacob and Esau

Once again we learn that it is God's decision to choose the descendants of His everlasting covenant. God chose Isaac, not Ishmael, and He chose Jacob, not Esau.

Chapter 7
SURVIVAL IN EGYPT

To understand the history of Israel we must remember that the hatred of the sons of Jacob for their brother Joseph that brought about the decision to sell him to slave traders that would bring Joseph into Egypt. Genesis 37:23-36 tells the story of how Joseph was sold to some Ishmaelite traders for 20 pieces of silver, and was brought by Midianites to Potiphar, the captain of the guard for Pharaoh himself.

It is so true that life brings unexpected changes and circumstances that at first seem difficult and unwanted. But God is working His wonderful plan even when we are not aware of what He is doing.

The story of Joseph is an amazing example of how God works in the lives of His people. Joseph will go from prison to the palace!

It was specifically a famine that brought Jacob and his family to Egypt. According to Genesis 50:19-21, Joseph spoke of how God was behind it all:

> "And Joseph said unto them, Fear not: for am I
> in the place of God? But as for you, ye thought
> evil against me; but God meant it unto good, to
> bring to pass, as it is this day, to save much people
> alive. Now therefore fear ye not: I will nourish
> you, and your little ones. And he comforted them,
> and spake kindly unto them."

But, the day came when (Exodus 1:8) a new ruler came to power in Egypt who knew not Joseph, but was threatened by the growth and power of the children of Israel.

Exodus 1:13-14 says: "And the Egyptians made the children of Israel to serve with rigor: And they made their lives bitter with hard bondage, in mortar, and in brick, and in all manner of service in the field; all their service, wherein they made them serve, was with rigor."

The king (Pharaoh) tried to kill all the Jewish baby boys. But, God used some midwives to protect them because they "feared God."

The children of Israel spent 400 years in bondage to Egypt. We read a significant fact about God's covenant in Exodus 2:23-25:

> "And it came to pass in process of time, that the
> king of Egypt died; and the children of Israel
> sighed by reason of the bondage, and they cried,
> and their cry came up unto God by reason of the
> bondage. And God heard their groaning, and God

remembered His covenant with Abraham, with Isaac, and with Jacob. And God looked upon the children of Israel, and God had respect unto them."

Yes, even in bondage to Egypt, God NEVER canceled His covenant!

The story of God's great deliverance of His people from the bondage of Egypt begins with a Levite couple who bore a child named Moses. They hid the child for three months, and eventually put the child in a little ark of bulrushes by the river's edge.

It was the *"daughter of Pharaoh"* who found the child and took him into her own palace and raised him to be the Pharaoh of Egypt in the future.

Many Bible scholars and teachers believe that the exodus from Egypt took place in 1446 BC, much earlier than some modern scholars of today put it.

It is also very possible that this *"daughter of Pharaoh"* was none other than Queen Hatshepsut whose funerary temple has been uncovered in the city of the dead on the west side of the Nile River at Luxor, Egypt.

Exodus 6:1-8 is wonderful encouragement to the people of Israel who were suffering under the severe bondage of Egypt.

"Then the LORD said unto Moses, Now shalt thou see what I will do to Pharaoh; for with a

strong hand shall he let them go, and with a strong hand shall he drive them out of his land. And God spake unto Moses, and said unto him, I am the LORD: And I appeared unto Abraham, unto Isaac, and unto Jacob, by the name of God Almighty, but by My Name JEHOVAH was I not known to them. And I have also established My covenant with them, to give them the land of Canaan, the land of their pilgrimage, wherein they were strangers. And I have also heard the groaning of the children of Israel, whom the Egyptians keep in bondage; and I have remembered My covenant. Wherefore say unto the children of Israel, I am the LORD, and I will bring you out from under the bondage of the Egyptians, and I will rid you out of their bondage, and I will redeem you with a stretched out arm, and with great judgments: And I will take you to Me for a people, and I will be to you a God: and ye shall know that I am the LORD your God, which bringeth you out from under the burdens of the Egyptians. And I will bring you in unto the land, concerning the which I did swear to Abraham, to Isaac, and to Jacob; and I will give it you for an heritage: I am the LORD."

The above words assure us all that no matter what happened to the children of Israel, God would NEVER cancel His covenant that He made with Abraham, Isaac, and

Jacob. That covenant promised a land, and God promises to bring them into that land.

The story of how God delivered His people from the bondage of Egypt, is remembered every year by Jewish people all around the world at the Feast of Passover and Unleavened Bread.

When the Jewish people put the blood of a sacrificial lamb on the top of their door and on the side posts of that door, the death angel "passed over" that home and did not kill the firstborn son. They were "redeemed" from their bondage and set free to enter the promised land.

After crossing the sea (Gulf of Aqaba) and seeing how God destroyed the army of Pharaoh, we read these words in Exodus 14:30-31:

> *"Thus the LORD saved Israel that day out of the hand of the Egyptians; and Israel saw the Egyptians dead upon the sea shore. And Israel saw that great work which the LORD did upon the Egyptians; and the people feared the LORD, and believed the LORD, and his servant Moses."*

Chapter 8
40 YEARS IN THE DESERT

A brief commentary on the "wilderness wanderings" of the children of Israel is found in the Book of Hebrews. In Hebrews 3:8-13 we read this:

> "Harden not your hearts, as in the provocation, in the day of temptation in the wilderness; When your fathers tempted Me, proved Me, and saw My works forty years. Wherefore I was grieved with that generation, and said, They do always err in their heart; and they have not known My ways. So I sware in My wrath, They shall not enter into My rest. Take heed, brethren, lest there be in any of you an evil heart of unbelief, in departing from the living God. But exhort one another daily, while it is called Today; lest any of you be hardened through the deceitfulness of sin."

Having visited those desert regions many times on trips to Israel, I have observed its desolation, heat, and difficult environment. If you simply walked from Egypt up to the present city of Beersheba, it would take you about two weeks! The children of Israel spent 40 years in that awful desert because of one simple fact — they "*hardened*" their "*hearts.*"

In spite of the rebellious attitudes and ungodly responses, God NEVER cancelled His covenant that He made with Abraham, Isaac, and Jacob.

Deuteronomy 1:31-32 tells us what was really wrong with the generation that wandered for 40 years in the wilderness:

> "*And in the wilderness, where thou hast seen how that the LORD thy God bare thee, as a man doth bear his son, in all the way that ye went, until ye came into this place. Yet in this thing ye did not believe the LORD your God.*"

There's the problem — they simply did not believe the LORD their God! That generation perished, and never went into the promised land. It was their children who went into the land under Joshua.

In spite of the unbelief of the children of Israel, the LORD God could keep His promise based on His covenant with Abraham, Isaac, and Jacob.

To the children of that generation that perished in the wilderness, God gave these instructions in Deuteronomy 4:1:

"Now therefore hearken, O Israel, unto the statutes and unto the judgments, which I teach you, for to do them, that ye may live, and go in and possess the land which the LORD God of your fathers giveth you."

Deuteronomy 4:31 says:

"For the LORD thy God is a merciful God; He will not forsake thee, neither destroy thee, nor forget the covenant of thy fathers which He sware unto them."

Once again it is clear that God will NEVER forsake His people nor FORGET His covenant that He made with Abraham, Isaac, and Jacob.

Deuteronomy 6:22-23 adds:

"And the LORD shewed signs and wonders, great and sore, upon Egypt, upon Pharaoh, and upon all his household, before our eyes: And He brought us out from thence, that He might bring us in, to give us the land which He sware unto our fathers."

The LORD urged His people to remember what He had done for them during those forty years. Deuteronomy 8:1-5 tells us:

"All the commandments which I command thee this day shall ye observe to do, that ye may live, and multiply, and go in and possess the land which

*the LORD sware unto your fathers. And thou
shalt remember all the way which the LORD thy
God led thee these forty years in the wilderness,
to humble thee, and to prove thee, to know what
was in thine heart, whether thou wouldest keep
His commandments or no. And He humbled
thee, and suffered thee to hunger, and fed thee with
manna, which thou knewest not, neither did thy
fathers know; that He might make thee know that
man doth not live by bread only, but by every word
that proceedeth out of the mouth of the LORD
doth man live. Thy raiment waxed not old upon
thee, neither did thy foot swell, these forty years.
Thou shalt also consider in thine heart, that, as
a man chasteneth his son, so the LORD thy God
chasteneth thee."*

God took care of His people in the most dreadful of
circumstances. His miraculous hand was supplying every
need they had.

The LORD reminded His people of what they were like
in that desert for 40 years. In Deuteronomy 9:7 we read:

*"Remember, and forget not, how thou provokedst
the LORD thy God to wrath in the wilderness:
from the day that thou didst depart out of the land
of Egypt, until ye came unto this place, ye have
been rebellious against the LORD."*

But, in spite of their rebellion, God NEVER cancelled His everlasting covenant that He made with Abraham, Isaac, Jacob, and their physical descendants!

Chapter 9
CONQUEST OF THE LAND

This amazing story starts with the servant of Moses, one of the two spies who challenged the children of Israel to trust God and not be afraid of the "giants" in the Land.

After the death of Moses, Joshua takes over as leader of Israel. In Joshua 1:2 we read:

> "Moses my servant is dead; now therefore arise, go over this Jordan, thou, and all this people, unto the land which I do give to them, even to the children of Israel."

The LORD promised Joshua that He would be with him all the days of his life, saying in Joshua 1:5-6: "*I will not fail thee, not forsake thee. Be strong and of a good courage: for unto this people shalt thou divide for an inheritance the land, which I sware unto their fathers to give them.*" Once again God brings up His covenant with Abraham, Isaac, and Jacob.

ISRAEL: Chosen by God

There were seven nations who were living in the Land when the children of Israel started their conquest at Jericho (Joshua 3:10):

- ✦ Canaanites
- ✦ Hittites
- ✦ Hivites
- ✦ Perizzites
- ✦ Girgashites
- ✦ Amorites
- ✦ Jebusites

According to Joshua 12:24 there were 31 pagan kings that needed to be conquered.

In Joshua's farewell address to the people we read in Joshua 24:14-15:

> *"Now therefore fear the LORD, and serve Him in sincerity and in truth: and put away the gods which your fathers served on the other side of the flood, and in Egypt; and serve ye the LORD. And if it seem evil unto you to serve the LORD, choose you this day whom ye will serve; whether the gods which your fathers served that were on the other side of the flood, or the gods of the Amorites, in whose land ye dwell: But as for me and my house, we will serve the LORD."*

In Judges 2:1 we read:

> *"And an angel of the LORD came up from Gilgal to Bochim, and said, I made you to go up out of Egypt, and have brought you unto the land which I*

sware unto your fathers; and I said, I will NEVER break My covenant with you."

Stronger words could not be spoken to convince all who would read the Bible that God's covenant is unconditional, everlasting, and will NEVER be cancelled!

According to the Bible (Judges 2:7) the children of Israel served the LORD all the days of Joshua, and all the days of the elders that outlived Joshua *"who had seen all the great works of the LORD, that He did for Israel."*

Joshua, the servant of the LORD, died at age 110 years.

Chapter 10
THE TIME OF JUDGES

The history of Israel is filled with conquest as well as conflict. The covenant of God was secure, based on God's love and faithfulness for His people, the people He had chosen for Himself.

The days of Joshua were days of victory and conquest, and the people actively served the LORD and experienced His blessing.

However, after the death of Joshua and the elders who served with him, Israel quickly changed!

Judges 2:10 says:

"and there arose another generation after them, which knew not the LORD, not yet the works which He had done for Israel."

Verses 11-13 state:

"And the children of Israel did evil in the sight of the LORD, and served Baalim: And they forsook the LORD God of their fathers, which brought

them out of the land of Egypt, and followed other gods, of the gods of the people that were round about them, and bowed themselves unto them, and provoked the LORD to anger. And they forsook the LORD, and served Baal and Ashtaroth."

One generation passed away, and the next one *"did evil in the sight of the LORD."*

God's anger was *"hot against Israel"* (Judges 2:14) and he allowed the nations around them to oppress them and put them into bondage once again.

Verse 16 says:

"Nevertheless the LORD raised up judges, which delivered them out of the hand of those that spoiled them."

But, when the judge died, Israel corrupted themselves again. God's judgment upon them was to let the nations they were to conquer to remain as a test to Israel.

The entire time of the judges was similar — the judge delivers them, but as soon as he died, Israel served other gods and did evil in the sight of the LORD.

A sad summary is made at the end of the Book of Judges (21:25) where we read these solemn words:

"In those days there was no king in Israel: every man did that which was right in his own eyes."

THE JUDGES

OTHNIEL

EHUD

SHAMGAR

DEBORAH/BARAK

GIDEON

TOLA

JAIR

JEPHTHAH

IBZAN

ELON

ABDON

SAMSON

Chapter 11
THE UNITED KINGDOM

It began with the prophet Samuel, the child of Hannah, the woman who was barren, and prayed for a child and God answered her prayer. The priest was Eli, and he had two wicked sons whom he would not discipline. These boys, Hophni and Phinehas, were guilty of violating their role as priests, and were guilty of sexual sin (I Samuel 2:22).

God promised to raise up a *"faithful priest"* to replace the family of Eli.

When the Philistines attacked and captured the Ark of the Covenant, the news brought the death of Eli and his two sons, and the birth of the child of Phinehas' wife who was named "Ichabod" which means "the glory has departed."

The Ark of the Covenant was in the country of the Philistines for seven months, and eventually comes to the house of Abinadab and put under the care of Eleazar his son. It stayed there for 20 years.

ISRAEL: Chosen by God

In I Samuel 7:3, Samuel the prophet exhorted the house of Israel with these words:

> *"If ye do return unto the LORD with all your hearts, then put away the strange gods and Ashtaroth from among you, and prepare your hearts unto the LORD, and serve Him only: and He will deliver you out of the hand of the Philistines."*

Soon the people wanted a king like other nations. In spite of the warning of Samuel, I Samuel 8:19 says:

> *"Nevertheless the people refused to obey the voice of Samuel; and they said, Nay; but we will have a king over us."*

They wanted Saul, the son of Kish from the tribe of Benjamin. He was *"a choice young man, and a goodly"* and no one was taller!

Saul had moments when the LORD touched him and used him for His glory. However, for most of his reign of 40 years, Saul was carnal, self-centered, often angry, and felt threatened by a little shepherd boy named David who could play the harp beautifully and was called *"the sweet psalmist of Israel"* (II Samuel 23:1).

The story of how David was chosen is indeed remarkable. He was anointed by the prophet Samuel. Under David, the warrior king, Israel enjoyed conquest and captured territory that gave them the largest kingdom they had in their history.

The Bible calls David *"a man after God's own heart."* His name appears more in the Bible than any other (except the LORD, of course!) The story of David is both thrilling and challenging. David committed adultery with Bathsheba, and set up the murder of her husband Uriah.

Who can forget the story of David and Goliath! Children around the world have enjoyed hearing how one little stone from David's sling slew the giant!

David reigned for 40 years, and there is hardly another man in history who fascinates us any more than King David.

The LORD God promised David that a descendant would come from his line who would rule the world. The promised Messiah was known among the Jewish people as *"the son of David."*

David's son, Nathan, was the ancestor of Miryam (Mary, mother of Jesus). The prophecy of Psalm 132:11 requires that the Messiah would come out of a Jewish woman in the line of King David.

But, the right to the throne comes through the line of David's son, Solomon, Israel's third king who reigned for 40 years like David.

Joseph who was betrothed (engaged) to Mary was in the direct line of Israel's kings. However, at the time of Coniah (Jechoniah) that line was cursed by God and could not bring us the promised Messiah.

Isaiah 9:6 says: *"For unto us a child is born, and unto us a son is given..."* The Messiah would come by birth and adoption. His birth brought Him out of the womb of a Jewish woman in King David's line — a virgin as the prophecy said (Isaiah 7:14). His adoption resulted from the marriage of Joseph to Mary after the birth of Yeshua (Jesus), and Joseph was in the line of the kings from King David. What a marvelous fact!

David's son, Solomon, is a wonderful example of God's blessing and fulfillment of God's promises.

Because his father, David, was a man of war and bloodshed, he was not allowed to build the Temple of the Lord, even though he raised the necessary resources to do so. Solomon was chosen by God to build this marvelous structure that would be Israel's place of worship for almost 400 years.

The United Kingdom lasted for 120 years with three kings ruling — Saul, David, and Solomon.

Chapter 12
THE DIVIDED KINGDOM

U nder the leadership of Solomon's son, Rehoboam, the unity of the kingdom was destroyed, and the rebellion of Jeroboam, son of Nebat, took ten tribes out of the original 12, and formed a coalition that would be known as "Israel" for over 200 years. The remaining two tribes, Judah and Benjamin, would now be called after the largest tribe — "Judah" and they would last for about 400 years.

All the kings of the northern coalition are described as wicked and idolatrous in their practices.

- ✦ JEROBOAM — 22 years
- ✦ NADAB — 2 years
- ✦ BAASHA — 24 years
- ✦ ELAH — 2 years
- ✦ ZIMRI — 7 days
- ✦ OMRI — 12 years
- ✦ AHAB — 22 years

- ✦ AHAZIAH — 2 years
- ✦ JEHORAM — 12 years
- ✦ JEHU — 28 years
- ✦ JEHOAHAZ — 17 years
- ✦ JEHOASH — 16 years
- ✦ JEROBOAM II — 41 years
- ✦ ZECHARIAH — 6 months
- ✦ SHALLUM — 1 month
- ✦ MENAHEM — 10 years
- ✦ PEKAHIAH — 2 years
- ✦ PEKAH — 20 years
- ✦ HOSHEA — 9 years

The Assyrian Empire attacked after several intrusions into the northern coalition, and in 722 BC they took the ten northern tribes of "Israel" into captivity. Judah was still in existence and would be in the land for another 130 years.

The kings of Judah sometimes did *"right in the sight of the LORD"* but not always.

- ✦ REHOBOAM –17 years
- ✦ ABIJAM — 3 years
- ✦ ASA — 41 years
- ✦ JEHOSHAPHAT — 25 years

- ✦ JEHORAM — 8 years
- ✦ AHAZIAH — 1 year
- ✦ ATHALIAH (mother — 6 years)
- ✦ JEHOASH — 40 years
- ✦ AMAZIAH — 29 years
- ✦ AZARIAH — 52 years
- ✦ JOTHAM — 16 years
- ✦ AHAZ — 16 years
- ✦ HEZEKIAH — 29 years

The following was said about Hezekiah, King of Judah, who was reigning in Judah when Assyria took the ten northern tribes into captivity (II Kings 18:3-7):

> "And he did that which was right in the sight of the LORD, according to all that David his father did. He removed the high places, and brake the images, and cut down the groves, and brake in pieces the brazen serpent that Moses had made: for unto those days the children of Israel did burn incense to it: and he called it Nehushtan. He trusted in the LORD God of Israel; so that after him was none like him among all the kings of Judah, nor any that were before him. For he clave to the LORD, and departed not from following Him, but kept His commandments, which the LORD commanded Moses. And the LORD was with him,

and he prospered withersoever he went forth: and he rebelled against the king of Assyria, and served him not."

✦ MANASSEH — 55 years

✦ AMON — 2 years

✦ JOSIAH — 31 years

✦ JEHOAHAZ — 3 months

✦ JEHOIAKIM (Eliakim) — 11 years

✦ JEHOIACHIN — 3 months

The King of Babylon (Nebuchadnezzar) attacked and eventually took Judah captive to Babylon and destroyed Jerusalem and the Temple of Solomon in 586 BC.

✦ MATTANIAH Zedekiah) — 11 years

He did *"evil in the sight of the LORD"* and his rebellion against the King of Babylon is what brought Jerusalem and the Temple of Solomon destruction.

A few Jews were left in the land by Babylon and Gedaliah was made the local ruler in behalf of Babylon.

The history of the divided kingdom brought both good and evil. The children of Israel renounced idolatry and immorality at times, but during much of this history, the pagan practices of the nations surrounding them became the practice of God's people. It is no wonder that God's judgment fell upon the northern coalition by Assyria and

the southern kingdom by Babylon. The Bible is replete with the details and there is no doubt about it — God judged His people severely for their sin and disobedience.

However, He NEVER cancelled or changed His covenant with Abraham, Isaac, and Jacob!

Chapter 13
DAYS OF CAPTIVITY

Assyria decided to marry the Israeli captives to their own women, and place these people back in the land. This fulfilled a specific prophecy in the Bible about the removal of the ten northern tribes from their place and position in God's prophetic plans.

The Samaritans were the result of this intermarriage, and as the New Testament says *"the Jews have no dealings with the Samaritans."*

But, our Lord Yeshua went to Samaria and many of the Samaritans became believers in observing and hearing about His credentials as Messiah!

Sometimes we hear folks speak of the "lost tribes of Israel" — the ones who went into captivity to Assyria. But, they are not "lost" to the mind and plans of our LORD! He has not forgotten them nor forsaken them!

The Bible tells us a great deal about the captivity of Judah to Babylon.

The words of the prophet Micah who prophesied in the days of Jotham, Ahaz, and Hezekiah — found at the end of his prophecy — Micah 7:18-20:

> *"Who is a God like unto Thee, that pardoneth iniquity, and passeth by the transgression of the remnant of His heritage? He retaineth not His anger forever, because He delighteth in mercy. He will turn again, He will have compassion upon us; He will subdue our iniquities; and Thou wilt cast all their sins into the depths of the sea. Thou wilt perform the truth to Jacob, and the mercy to Abraham, which Thou hast sworn unto our fathers from the days of old."*

What wonderful encouragement this passage is! God's covenant remains in spite of their sin!

These words were essential for the children of Israel and Judah to hear. First Assyria, then Babylon, will attack and take many into captivity — but God's covenant will NOT change! It is NOT dependent upon human performance or merit!

The Assyrian Empire fell into the hands of the Babylonians when the great city of Nineveh fell in 612 BC. It would be only 26 years and Babylon would destroy Jerusalem and the Temple of Solomon. The southern kingdom of Judah would go into captivity for 70 years.

The Bible has much to say about Babylon. We find the word 286 times in the Bible of which 12 times are found in the New Testament, and six of those in the Book of Revelation.

Most of the references about Babylon refer to the massive and beautiful city of the Neo-Babylonian period (625-539 BC). With its "Hanging Gardens" and massive walls it was regarded as one of the "Seven Wonders of the Ancient World."

Ancient Babylon covered an area of 1,000 acres making it the largest city of the ancient world, some 15% larger than Nineveh. It had 1,179 temples and a population of over 100,000, but could easily have handled over 250,000 people.

The famous "Ishtar Gate" was 70 feet high and 15 feet wide. Over 6,000 idols were uncovered in the excavations of ancient Babylon and over 10 major altars. There were 180 open-air shrines for Ishtar and 200 identifiable places for other deities.

The ziggurat (tower) named Etemenanki was called "the foundation house of heaven and earth." It measured about 300 feet square at its base and rose in seven stages to a height of 300 feet.

It could very well have been restored and reconstructed from the original "Tower of Babel" mentioned in Genesis 11. The Babylonians believed it was built by the gods.

According to Genesis 10:8-10 the story of Babylon began with a man named "Nimrod" whose name means "to revolt or rebel." His wife's name was "Semiramis" — the first high priestess of the Babylonian mystery religion.

The prophet Jeremiah speaks volumes about Babylon, the captivity of Judah, and the eventual fall of this city and empire. Many of the verses in Jeremiah are found in Revelation 17-18 where Babylon the Great is a woman riding a seven-headed beast with ten horns on the seventh head. Babylon is called the "Mother of harlots and abominations" — Babylonianism is both religious and political. Babylon the Great is also called a "mystery."

The Book of Lamentations is connected to the Book of Jeremiah in the Hebrew Bible, and properly so. It reveals the weeping and mourning of the few remaining Jews in Jerusalem over the terrible destruction of Jerusalem and its Temple. Lamentations 3:22-23 is a great blessing to these discouraged people:

> "It is of the LORD's mercies that we are not consumed, because His compassions fail not. They are new every morning; great is Thy faithfulness."

Verses 31-32 add:

> "For the LORD will not cast off forever; But though He cause grief, yet will He have compassion according to the multitude of His mercies."

Chapter 13: DAYS OF CAPTIVITY

God's mercy was there even in the terrible days of conquest by Babylon and the subsequent captivity of the Jewish people.

Chapter 14
PERSIAN HELP

We read in Isaiah 45 that a great king of ancient Persia named Cyrus would be a special servant of the Lord — called *"His Annointed."* Cyrus is the one God used to return His people to the Land of promise and blessing.

There is a great deal of history about ancient Persia and its relationship to Israel. The books of Nehemiah, Esther, and Daniel tell us a great deal.

Nehemiah was the cup bearer to King Artaxerxes Longimanus, and was granted the privilege to return to the ruins of Jerusalem and rebuild the wall. That decree by a Persian king is dated for us in Nehemiah 2:1 — *"in the month Nisan, in the twentieth year of Artaxerxes the king."* Daniel 9:25 mentions this decree as the beginning point of "seventy weeks" or "seventy sevens (490 years)." The 20th year of King Artaxerxes Longimanus was 445 BC.

In the Book of Esther, the Persian king is called *"Aha-suerus."* Scholars have overwhelmingly identified him as the famous Xerxes of Persian history. He came to power in 485 BC and ruled to 465 BC. He was succeeded by his son Artaxerxes Longimanus I (the one mentioned in the Book of Nehemiah).

Xerxes was the son of Darius the Great and Atossa, the daughter of Cyrus the Great (Isaiah 45) — the one who allowed the Jews to return to Israel to rebuild the city and temple.

Xerxes is the one who made a massive attack against the Grecians and Spartans with two million men (Herodotus says!), including 10,000 elite warriors named "Persian Immortals." His battle with 300 Spartans delayed his advance upon Athens. When Xerxes finally arrived in Athens, it was totally deserted. Xerxes ordered the burning of Athens, but a day later he regretted it, and issued an order to rebuild it. Xerxes is also the one who completed the building projects at Susa (Hebrew — "Shushan") and Persepolis which his father Darius had begun.

The Bible correctly and accurately says that Xerxes ruled *"from India even unto Ethiopia."* His father, Darius I, is the one who conquered India, and Cambyses, who ruled from 530-522 BC, is the one who conquered Ethiopia (today's Egypt and Sudan). To control this vast empire, it was divided into 127 provinces. Daniel 6:1-3 refers to the

rule of Xerxes' father, Darius the Mede, who set up these provinces as the Bible accurately says — *"over the kingdom."* Those who managed these provinces were called *"princes"* and three *"presidents"* were in charge of overseeing the work of the *"princes."* Daniel was the favorite *"president"* of King Darius and the king planned to make him *"over the whole realm."* Daniel 6:28 tells us: *"So this Daniel prospered in the reign of Darius and in the reign of Cyrus the Persian."*

What is fascinating to students of history is that ancient Persia (whom God used to be a blessing to His people Israel) was originally the country of Elam (son of Shem — Genesis 10:22). Since 1979, Persia became the Islamic Republic of Iran and its leaders make boastful threats as to how they are going to "wipe Israel off of the map"!

Psalm 83 speaks of how the enemies of Israel *"have taken crafty counsel against Thy people, and consulted against Thy hidden ones. They have said, Come, and let us cut them off from being a nation; that the name of Israel may be no more in remembrance. For they have consulted together with one consent: they are confederate against Thee."* Israel has faced such hostility in the past, but God's covenant will NOT be cancelled or forsaken!

God can use any of the nations of the world to be a blessing to Israel.

Psalm 76:10 says: *"Surely the wrath of man shall praise Thee: the remainder of wrath shalt Thou restrain."* Proverbs

21:1 adds: *"The king's heart is in the hand of the LORD, as the rivers of water: He turneth it whithersoever He will."*

There are still many Iranians who love and support Israel in spite of their government's attitudes and actions. Never forget — the LORD GOD of ISRAEL is still in control!

Chapter 15
GREEK DOMINATION

Daniel 8:20-25 tells us a very accurate account of the history that deeply affected the Land of Israel and its people. It was a vision given to Daniel the prophet:

> "The ram which thou sawest having two horns are the kings of Media and Persia. And the rough goat is the King of Greece: and the great horn that is between his eyes is the first King. Now that being broken, whereas four stood up for it, four kingdoms shall stand up out of the nation, but not in his power. And in the latter time of their kingdom, when the transgressors are come to the full, a king of fierce countenance, and understanding dark sentences, shall stand up. And his power shall be mighty, but not by his own power; and he shall destroy wonderfully, and shall prosper, and practice, and shall destroy the mighty and the holy people."

As Daniel saw, the *"rough goat is the King of Greece."* The *"first King"* is none other than Alexander the Great. History records the amazing story of his conquests. Very few in history have ever accomplished what Alexander did, especially at the speed in which he did it.

When Alexander died, with no more worlds to conquer, his kingdom was divided up into his four generals:

+ LYSIMACHUS
+ CASSANDER
+ SELEUCID
+ PTOLEMY

From Daniel 11 and from secular history we know that both the Seleucid and Ptolemy dynasties fought continually over the Land of Israel. From an historical point of view, Daniel 11 is an amazing and accurate listing of those conflicts, involving the kingdoms of Syria and Egypt.

According to the Bible, *"a king of fierce countenance"* would come on the scene and cause much violence to the Land of Israel and its people. The Temple had been rebuilt (although nothing like what Solomon had done!) and the sacrificial system reinstituted.

Daniel 11:36 refers to this *"king of fierce countenance"* as *"the king"* who will *"do according to his will."* In verses 36-39 we learn about this coming king:

"...he shall exalt himself, and magnify himself above every god, and shall speak marvelous things against the GOD of gods, and shall prosper till the indignation be accomplished: for that that is determined shall be done. Neither shall he regard the God of his fathers, nor the desire of women, nor regard any god: for he shall magnify himself above all. But in his estate shall he honor the God of forces; and a god whom his fathers knew not shall he honor with gold, and silver, and precious stones, and pleasant things. Thus shall he do in the most strong holds with a strange god, whom he shall acknowledge and increase with glory: and he shall cause them to rule over many, and shall divide the land for gain."

His name? ANTIOCHUS EPIPHANES IV

In John 10:22 we read that Yeshua attended *"the feast of dedication"* in Jerusalem and *"it was winter."*

Today, Jews around the world celebrate the festival known as Hanukkah. The central focus is a Menorah with nine candles rather than the seven candles of the Temple Menorah. The central candle of the Hanukkah Menorah represents the Messiah. Isaiah 42:1-16 speaks of the Messiah as God's covenant to the Gentiles. Verse 6 calls Him *"a light of the Gentiles."* The eight branches of the Hanukkah Menorah represent how the LORD sustained

the oil that gave light to the Temple while a special family called "Maccabees" cleansed the Temple of the pagan influence under Antiochus Epiphanes IV.

THE DETAILS ABOUT HANUKKAH

(Thanks to the "Jesus Boat" friends in Galilee for this fine article!)

When Alexander the Great died, his Empire was divided amongst his generals. The Land of Israel was given to Seleucid. For over 100 years the Jews were afforded much of the same privileges and rights as other citizens of the Empire. However, Antiochus III, the great-great grandson of Seleucid, was forced to fight a costly war against the Romans.

As a result the Jewish people fell out of favor with Antiochus III and thus the beginning of the end of equality for the Jews.

In 174 BCE Antiochus III's son, Antiochus IV, began his reign over the Empire. He was a harsh and cruel king; a tyrant of reckless nature and contemptuous of religions and customs that were not his own.

Antiochus IV wanted to unite his kingdom under his religion, which was the worship of the Greek idol Zeus. Within the Empire he stifled all Jewish Law. He removed the righteous High Priest Yochanan from the Temple

in Jerusalem. Yochanan was replaced with his brother Joshua — a Hellenistic Jew who called himself by the Greek name Jason. Jason used his position as High Priest to infect the priesthood and the Jewish people with the traditions and religion of the Greeks. Jason was soon replaced by another named Menelaus who defiled the Temple with the worship of Greek idols.

Yochanan was outraged by his brother's behavior and that of Menelaus. When Antiochus IV was away fighting a war against Egypt Yochanan began to rally the Jews to disobey the new customs and religion being forced on them. The Jewish people were afraid of Antiochus' reprisals and mostly did nothing. However, when the Romans spread a rumor that Antiochus IV had been killed, the Jewish people rebelled against Menelaus causing him to flee.

Much to the horror of the Jews, Antiochus returned from battle alive and enraged by Roman meddling and Jewish rebellion. He ordered his army to strike out against the Jews killing thousands. Antiochus IV then ordered a series of extremely harsh decrees against the Jewish people and religion.

All Jewish worship was forbidden. All Scrolls of the Law were confiscated and burned.

Observation of the Shabbat, was prohibited under penalty of death. As the soldiers went town to town ravaging the Land of Israel they forced Jewish inhabitants to

worship their pagan idols and eat the flesh of pigs. Many complied, but some refused and died for their beliefs.

One day Antiochus' soldiers arrived in a town called Modiin just outside Jerusalem. An old, great priest named Mattiyahu was an inhabitant of this town. The soldiers built an altar to their pagan idols in the center of town and ordered Mattiyahu to worship at it.

Mattiyahu refused. A Hellenistic Jew approached the altar to offer a sacrifice. Mattiyahu took out his sword and killed him, and his sons and neighbors sprang on the Greek soldiers killing or chasing them away. Mattiyahu knew when Antiochus IV heard of this rebellion there would be a heavy price to pay. He fled together with his sons and neighbors to the hills of Judah. Here they lived in the caves and encouraged all loyal and courageous Jews to join them. They formed legions and would carefully leave the caves to attack outposts of Greek and Syrian soldiers and destroy pagan altars.

When old Mattiyahu was on his deathbed, he called his sons together. He encouraged them to defend God's Torah. He asked that the tactical leader be Shimon the Wise and in battle the leader be Judah the Strong. Judah was known as Maccabee — a contraction for "Mi Kamocha Ba'eilim HaShem" translated as "Who is like you, O God." This was sung to God by Moses and the Israelites after God parted the Red Sea giving them safe passage and destroying the Egyptians (Exodus 15:11). Judah's follow-

ers became known as "The Maccabees" and caused great havoc to the Empire.

Eventually Antiochus sent one of his best generals to wipe out this little band of Jewish fighters. Even though the Empire's army was much better equipped and greater in number, the Maccabees were triumphant in battle again and again.

Antiochus IV realized that he needed to put an end to this rebellion once and for all. He sent an army of 40,000 men into the Judean hills. When Judah and the Maccabees heard the army coming they cried, "Let us fight to the death in defense of our souls and our Temple!" The Maccabees fought with God in their hearts and the honor of Judaism in their souls. They fought for their Torah and for their Temple. After a series of bloody battles, it was done. They had defeated the powerful army of Antiochus. With their victory, the Maccabees climbed a mountain outside Jerusalem and looked upon the city. On the 25th of Kislev they descended the mountain to liberate Jerusalem and reclaim their Temple. As they marched into the Holy City they were distressed by what they saw — idols, impurity, and filth everywhere. They entered the Holy Temple and were shocked to see the same. Jerusalem and the Temple needed to be made Holy again for God.

They began in the Temple, clearing it of all pagan idols and building a new altar. The golden Menorah had been stolen by the Syrians and Greeks so the Maccabees

made a new one from what they could find. They wanted the light of the Menorah to rededicate the Temple to the One True God. They rummaged through the ruins seeking a flask of sanctified oil, but all had been defiled. Finally, they found a small jug in which the Kohen seal was still intact. They carefully poured the oil into their makeshift Menorah even though they realized that there was only enough oil for one day. They also realized that it would take eight days to sanctify more oil for the Temple. Nevertheless, the Maccabees had faith and dedicated the Holy Temple and lit the Menorah.

Jewish tradition tells us that a great miracle occurred. The oil burned through the first night and on to the second, then on to the third. The oil continued to burn for eight nights until more oil was ready for the Temple. This miracle proved that God was with the Maccabees all along. They fought for what they believed and held fast in the face of death with God at their side. Their faith in God and the Torah never wavered and God showed them His Divine presence.

Those eight miraculous nights have been chosen as the commemoration of this miracle. Jewish people light the Hanukkah Menorah to show God their faith in Him, His Torah, and their beliefs and traditions.

The Greek domination of Israel affected many areas of Jewish life and practice. By the time of the New Testa-

ment, we read of Hellenistic Jews — those who assimilated into the culture.

Even during the time of Roman domination, Greek influence was everywhere. It had an enormous affect upon the Jewish people.

But, what followed the Greek empire was even more awesome upon the Jewish people — which brings us in our history to....

ROME!

Chapter 16
ROME AND 70 AD

Within this brief book, it is impossible to describe all that Rome was in its control and influence upon the Jewish people and the Land of Israel. What happened in 70 AD lives in its horror and violence upon Jewish hearts and minds still today. It is sad indeed that so few Christians know what really happened.

The Roman Republic began in 705 BC, but it was not until 30 BC that we read of the Roman Empire. The first Caesar was Octavian, the nephew of Julius Caesar. People today know him as "Augustus Caesar." Rome's first emperor. In 30 BC he proclaimed the "Pax Romana" — the so-called Roman peace over all the world. The New Testament not only speaks of him but gives details about his reign and influence in the Land of Israel.

One of the most important rulers in the days of the Roman Empire was Herod the Great, who along with his sons, takes "center stage" in the descriptions of history and in the New Testament.

WHO WAS HEROD THE GREAT?

(Thanks to Rabbi Ken Spiro for this excellent study!)

A madman who murdered his own family and a great many rabbis. Herod was also the greatest builder in Jewish history. Herod, the Great (not to be confused with Herod Antipas who came later) is one of the most important characters in Jewish history. He was ambitious, cruel and paranoid to be sure, but, nevertheless, he remains a very significant person in the terms of understanding this period of Roman domination of the Jewish people.

Herod's first leadership role was as governor of the Galilee, a position granted to him by his father, Antipater.

The background to Herod's rise to power is the Roman civil war that will transform Rome from a republic into an empire ruled by the Caesars or emperors. In 44 BC Julius Caesar is murdered by Brutus and Cassius who are in turn defeated by Antony and Octavian in 42 BC. The Battle of Actium in 31 BC is the final showdown between Octavian and Antony. Octavian emerged as the unrivaled victor, changing his name to Augustus and becoming the first Roman emperor.

Herod had originally sided with Antony but switches allegiance at the last minute and backs Octavian. His last minute support for Octavian earned him Augustus's confirmation as King of Israel.

Herod will reign as king of Judea from 37 BC until his death on January 14, 1 BC, a very long reign of over 35 years, and in many ways a good period in terms of development and building of the country and social stability. Part of the reason for the stability was that during this time, the Romans took a backseat role in the day-to-day life of the Jews.

The general Roman attitude was one of tolerance, meaning Jews were granted exemptions from the official Roman state religion. A very interesting point to remember is that religion and state went together in all empires in the ancient world, and more so in Rome than almost anywhere because Rome also practiced emperor worship — that is, the Romans deified their emperors posthumously.

Linking state and religion gave the rulers added legitimacy, obviously. The connection between temporal power and spiritual power gave them complete control over the physical existence and spiritual existence of their subjects. (Later, we see the Catholic Church doing the same thing in Medieval Europe.)

While accepting the state religion as a vital part of Roman identity and loyalty to the state, the Romans were also pragmatists. They had learned by the Greek experience that Jews could not be forced to worship idols. And they saw for themselves that the Jews were not like other pagan peoples — they were not going to conform. So the

Romans granted the Jews an official status of being exempt from Roman state religion.

On the one hand, it was a very smart and very tolerant policy. On the other hand, with that policy also went a punitive tax specifically for the Jews called "fiscus Judaicus." You want to be exempt from the state religion? Okay, so long as you pay for the privilege.

So, it might have happened that the Jews simply paid the tax and did their own thing. But it didn't go as smoothly as that.

Herod's rule was characterized by a period of unprecedented growth and construction, thanks in large part to Herod's amiable relationship with Rome and his obsession with massive and elaborate construction projects.

Herod had Rome's complete support in administering a very important territory which included several major trade routes. Everything moved through Judea, which was sort of like the great way-station for the incense trade coming from Yemen up the Arabian Peninsula and going out to the Mediterranean.

Additionally, this was one of the most agriculturally productive pieces of land in the Middle East famous for its olive oil (which was used as a main source of light, and not just for cooking), for its dates (the chief sweetener in the times before sugar), and for its wine.

Herod used the huge profits from trade and money acquired through the crushing taxes he placed upon his subjects to undertake a series of mammoth building projects — some of the most magnificent in the world.

As a matter of fact if they hadn't closed the list of the wonders of the ancient world before his time, Herod would probably have added three more to the list. Almost all archeologists and students of architecture of the ancient world appreciate that he was one of the greatest builders of all human history. He built relentlessly — cities, palaces and fortresses, some of which still stand: the fortresses at Masada, Antonia and Herodium, the port city of Caesarea Maritima, the huge edifice at the top of the Cave of the Patriarchs in Hebron, the massive fortifications around Jerusalem as well as three towers at the entrance to the city (the remains of which are today erroneously named the Tower of David) and much more.

At Herodium, in an incredible feat of engineering — Herod built an artificial mountain and, on top of it, a huge palace. Unfortunately, this palace was destroyed in 70 AD during the Great Revolt.

He built another fortress, Masada, on top of a rock plateau, in the desert. Complete with all the creature comforts in the desert, Masada had an incredible water supply system that fed gardens for growing agricultural staples and three bathhouses (Masada is open to tourists today and is a sight to behold.)

The port city of Caesarea Maritima deserves special mention — not only because it was a center of trade and the Roman administrative capitol of Judea and one of the largest ports in the Empire, but because it became a symbol in Jewish eyes of everything that was pagan, Roman, and antithetical to Judaism. Here Herod created an amazing artificial port (one of the two largest in the Empire), put in a beautiful amphitheater, a hippodrome for chariot races, bath houses, and a huge temple dedicated to the Roman god-emperor, Augustus Caesar.

The most ambitious of Herod's projects was the re-building of the Temple, which was almost certainly an attempt to gain popularity among his subjects who, he knew, held him in contempt and also to make amends for his cruelty toward the rabbis.

It took 10,000 men ten years just to build the retaining walls around the Temple Mount (on top of which the Muslim shrine, the Dome of the Rock, stands today). The Western Wall (formerly known as the Wailing Wall) is merely part of that 500-meter-long retaining wall that was designed to hold a huge man-made platform that could accommodate twenty- four football fields. When it was completed, it was the world's largest functioning

religious site and until today it remains the largest man-made platform in the world.

There's no question that Herod had a huge ego and liked to impress people with grandiose building projects. But there is also another more practical reason. Historians estimate that there were about 6-7 million Jews living in the Roman Empire (plus another 1 million in Persia), many of whom would come to Jerusalem for the three pilgrimage festivals: Passover, Shavuot (Pentecost) and Sukkot (Tabernacles). So you had to have a huge space to accommodate such a large number of people.

When it came to building the Temple itself on top of this platform, Herod truly outdid himself, and even the Talmud acknowledges that the end-result was spectacular. "He who has not seen Herod's building, has never in his life seen a truly grand building." (Talmud-Bava Basra 4a)

The Holy of Holies was covered in gold; the walls and columns of the other buildings were of white marble; the floors were of marble, its blue tinge giving the impression of a moving sea of water; the curtains were tapestries of blue, white, scarlet and purple thread, depicting, according to Josephus, "the whole vista of the heavens."

Josephus describes how incredible it looked: "Viewed from without, the Sanctuary had everything that could amaze either mind or eyes. Overlaid all round with stout

plates of gold, the first rays of the sun it reflected so fierce a blaze of fire that those who endeavored to look at it were forced to turn away as if they had looked straight at the sun. To strangers as they approached it seemed in the distance like a mountain covered with snow; for any part not covered with gold was dazzling white... (The Jewish War, p. 304)"

Herod saw fit, however, to place at the main entrance a huge Roman eagle, which the pious Jews saw as a sacrilege. A group of Torah students promptly smashed this emblem of idolatry and oppression, but Herod had them hunted down, dragged in chains to his residence in Jericho, where they were burned alive.

Having built the Temple, Herod took pains to make sure it would be run without future problems of this kind. He appointed his own High Priest, having by then put to death forty-six leading members of the Sanhedrin, the rabbinical court.

Herod's persecutions were infamous and they even extended to his own family. Herod, knowing that his Jewish credentials were suspect, had married Miriam — the granddaughter of Hyrcanus and therefore a Hasmonean princess — largely to gain legitimacy among the Jewish people. But he also loved her madly. As Josephus relates: "Of the five children which Herod had by Miriam, two of them were daughters and three were sons. The youngest of

these sons was educated in Rome and died there but the two eldest he treated as those of royal blood on account of the nobility of their mother and because they were not born until he was king. But what was stronger than all this was his love he bore for Miriam which inflamed him every day to a great degree."

The problem was that Miriam hated him as much as he loved her, largely because of what he had done to her brother, Aristobulus. Herod had made Aristobulus High Priest at the age of 17, and watched with trepidation as the young man became hugely popular. This was not surprising as Aristobulus was a Hasmonean with a legitimate right to be High Priest — a genuine Jew and a genuine "cohen." But this threatened Herod too much and he had him drowned.

Indeed, Herod later became jealous of his own sons for the same reason and had them murdered as well. And he even had his own wife murdered in a fit of jealousy.

Josephus again: "His passion also made him stark mad and leaping out of his bed he ran around the palace in a wild manner. His sister Salome took the opportunity also to slander Miriam and to confirm his suspicions about Joseph (Miriam's alleged lover). Then out of his ungovernable jealousy and rage he commanded both of them to be killed immediately. But as soon as his passion was over he repented of what he had done and as soon

as his anger had worn off his affections were kindled again ... Indeed, the flame of his desires for her was so hard that he could not think she was dead but he would appear under his disorders to speak to her as if she were still alive... (Antiquities 15.7.4,5)"

Not a stable man to say the least. Even Augustus said of him: "It is better to be Herod's dog than one of his children." Herod's paranoia, his interference with the Temple hierarchy, and his dedication to the Hellenization of the Jewish people all contributed to the growing discontent that would erupt in a revolt against Rome some 70 years after his death.

Beneath the surface events, there was a deeper spiritual battle raging — between paganism and Judaism. Additionally, Jewish nationalistic feelings were rising to the surface. It didn't help matters that Hellenism dominated Judea. A significant number of Greeks as well as other gentiles who adopted the Greek life-style had lived here since the days of the Greek Empire and now, encouraged by the Romans, more Hellenist outsiders came to settle the land. Additionally, the Jewish upper-classes, though a minority, subscribed to this "higher" culture. And of course, the king was an avowed Hellenist.

As a result of Herod's interference and the ever-spreading Hellenistic influences among the Jewish upper classes, the Temple hierarchy became very corrupt. The Saddu-

cees, a religious group of the wealthy, who collaborated with the Romans in order to keep their power base, now controlled the Temple, much to the chagrin of the mainstream Jewish majority, the Pharisees, and of the extreme religious minority, the Zealots. The cauldron was beginning to boil and soon it would erupt.

THE JEWISH REVOLT

In the spring of 66 AD, the Jews of Roman Judea had had enough of Roman intolerance and rose up in rebellion against the excesses of the procurator Gessius Florus.

Without any apparent plan or organized leadership, rebels seized control of Jerusalem section by section, and then finally massacred the sole cohort of Roman infantry left behind by Florus as a garrison. A relief army of 30,000 under Cestius Gallus, the Roman Governor of Syria, quickly quashed resistance in northern Judea and then marched on Jerusalem, assaulting the walls for eight days and seriously demoralizing the defenders before withdrawing (presumably because his army was proving unreliable and he lacked a siege train to conduct siege operations). Gallus retired to Beth-Horon, where the rejuvenated rebels attacked him, inflicting a heavy defeat. Realizing that the die was irreparably cast for war, the Jewish aristocrat and priest classes quickly organized the

country, dividing it into eleven administrative districts, each with its own commander and small army.

Unfortunately for their cause, the divided Jewish forces were unable to coordinate their operations or come to each for mutual support.

The Emperor Nero responded to news of Gallus' defeat by dispatching Vespasian to command the three legions and auxiliaries (nearly 60,000 men) already in route to suppress the rebellion. The Romans successfully besieged Jotapata and then marched to the port of Caesarea, where they met Vespasian, who led them across country to Tiberias and Gamla. This campaign successfully secured the Galilee by the close of 67 AD. Roman successes prompted internal dissension among the Jewish leaders, leading the fanatical Zealots under John and their allies, the Idumaean Jews of southern Judea, to overthrow the aristocrats and seize control of Jerusalem. Later, Simon and his bandits entered the city and contested the Zealots' control, making life doubly difficult for the aristocrats and priests.

Vespasian then moved southward in a multi-pronged campaign that resulted in the recapture of Gadara, Jericho and Emmaus, thus successfully isolating the Jewish rebels at Jerusalem by the close of 68 AD. Before he could complete the campaign, however, Nero was overthrown and Vespasian was proclaimed emperor by his eastern legions

in July 69 AD. Shortly thereafter, he departed for Rome, leaving his son Titus in command of operations.

Titus then moved on Jerusalem, which fell in September 70 AD, after a seven month siege. The Herodian temple and much of the city was razed, captives were shipped off to the gladiatorial games or Roman mines, and John and Simon were captured and sent to Rome to participate in Vespasian's Triumph, after which Simon was executed. The fall of Jerusalem marked the effective end of the Jewish Revolt, however mop-up operations continued for the next four years under the generals Lucilius Bassus and Flavius Silva against fanatical bands of rebels who holed up in fortresses at Herodium, Machaerus and Masada in the south of Judea. Masada was the last to fall (Spring 74 AD). After the Romans had completed extensive preparations for an assault against the rocky citadel, Masada's defenders committed mass suicide rather than risk falling into Roman hands.

The second Jewish Revolt (132-135 AD) was prompted by the Emperor Hadrian, who during his travels through Judea in 130 AD indulged himself in several provocations, including a decree banning circumcision, construction of a tomb to Pompey (who had desecrated the Temple of Yahweh in Jerusalem in 63 BC) and the pronouncement that he would rebuild Jerusalem as the Roman city Aeolia Capitolina, including construction of a temple to Jupiter

Capitolinus on the site of Herod's temple. Apparently designed to provoke a reaction, Hadrian's actions certainly did not sit well with the people, who promptly revolted under the leadership of Simon Bar Kokhba.

Little is recorded of the rebellion, despite the fact that it was fiercely fought and lasted approximately three and a half years before the Roman army under Julius Serverus was able to bring Bar Kokhba to bay in a fortress near Jerusalem. Jewish annals record that 50 forts and 985 villages were destroyed and that 580,000 Jews were killed during the course of the war. The Romans for their part were reputed to have lost one of their legions. In the rebellion's aftermath, Hadrian permanently banned Jews from setting foot in Jerusalem and then rebuilt the city as a Roman colony. A Jewish presence has remained in the Land of Israel since that time until the present day.

SO, DID GOD CANCEL HIS COVENANT?

This has become the opinion of many Bible teachers and scholars and it seriously undermines the Bible's teaching concerning Israel and the faithfulness of God to His everlasting covenant with Abraham, Isaac, and Jacob.

Those who believe this will also point to the fact that the entire Book of Revelation (in their opinion) was written before 70 AD. (Historical documentation is

totally lacking, and history confirms that the Book of Revelation was written in 95 AD!)

They also believe that the teaching of our Lord Yeshua (Olivet Discourse) confirms that the destruction of Jerusalem marks the end of God's plans for Israel.

They see the Second Coming of the Messiah as happening in 70 AD in the sense of God's judgment upon Israel. Frankly, such teaching is utter nonsense at best, and lacks completely in Biblical and historical evidence. God has NEVER cancelled His covenant and has NEVER forsaken His people!

Some answer this problem by insisting that the Church has replaced Israel in God's prophetic plan. (See the author's booklet entitled "REPLACEMENT THEOLOGY.")

Chapter 17
CHURCH HISTORY

After the events of the Book of Acts and the missionary journeys of the Apostle Paul, the story of the Jewish people throughout church history is not good.

The Church began in Jerusalem, not Rome, and the first pastor was Yaakov (James) not Peter. It was Jewish in belief and practice, and very Messianic, believing that Yeshua ben Yoseph was and is the true Messiah of Israel. A church council (Acts 15) made the decision to allow Gentiles to become members with Jews in the Church based on the teachings of the Hebrew prophets. Both Jews and Gentiles would become "one in Yeshua HaMashiach."

At the time of the 2nd Jewish revolt in the 2nd century AD, the pressure was upon Jewish people to believe that Bar Kokhba was the Messiah. Jewish believers in Yeshua could not do so, and so were considered to be "traitors." Thus began a serious division between Jewish people over the true identity of the Messiah.

It did not take long for church leaders to see the Jews as a threat to their leadership and beliefs. The verbal attacks began, and grew worse in time. A great orator and preacher named Chrysostom spoke out against Jews saying:

"The synagogue is worse than a brothel...it is the den of scoundrels and the repair of wild beasts...the temple of demons devoted to idolatrous cults.... the refuge of brigands and debauchees, and the cavern of devils. It is a criminal assembly of Jews...a place of meeting for the assassins of Christ...a house worse than a drinking shop...a den of thieves; a house of ill fame; a dwelling of iniquity, the refuge of devils, a gulf and abyss of perdition."

Chrysostom also said this about the Jewish people:

"As for me, I hate the synagogue....I hate the Jews for the same reason."

For many centuries the Jews heard these three words of St. John Chrysostom: *"God hates you."*

In a book by Edward Flannery entitled "THE ANGUISH OF THE JEWS" we read this quote by Raul Hillberg, scholar of the Holocaust:

"Since the 4ᵗʰ century AD there have been three anti-Jewish policies: (forced) conversion, expulsion, annihilation. The second appeared as an alternative to the first, and the third emerged as an alternative to the second. The missionaries of Christianity

had said in effect: You have no right to live among us as Jews. The secular rulers who followed proclaimed: You have no right to live among us. The Nazis at last decreed: You have no right to live.

The process began with the attempt to drive the Jews into Christianity. The development was continued in order to force the victims into exile. It was completed when the Jews were driven to their deaths. The German Nazis, then, did not discard the past; they built upon it. They did not begin a development, they completed it."

When the Protestant Reformation began, it owed much to the courage and boldness of Martin Luther, an Augustinian monk who defied the beliefs and practices of the Roman Church, and is known for the nailing of his 95 theses to the door of the church at Wittenberg, Germany.

But, it was Luther himself who wrote in 1543 AD:

"First, their synagogues should be set on fire…Secondly, their homes should likewise be broken down and destroyed…Thirdly, they should be deprived of their prayer-books and Talmuds…Fourthly, their rabbis must be forbidden under threat of death to teach any more…Fifthly, passport and traveling privileges should be absolutely forbidden to the Jews…Sixthly, they ought to be stopped from usury (charging interest on loans)*…Seventhly,*

let the young and strong Jews and Jewesses be given the flail, the ax, the hoe, the spade, the distaff, and spindle, and let them earn their bread by the sweat of their noses…We ought to drive the rascally lazy bones out of our system…Therefore away with them…To sum up, dear princes and nobles who have Jews in your domains, if this advice of mine does not suit you, then find a better one so that you and we may all be free of this insufferable devilish burden — the Jews."

Adolph Hitler made it very clear that he was dealing with the "Jewish problem" as Martin Luther suggested.

As Michael Brown states in his book "OUR HANDS ARE STAINED WITH BLOOD" on page 17:

"Let the saints and popes and Luther himself arise from their graves and weep. The Church has blood on her hands."

There are many fine books that deal with the persecution and execution of Jewish people throughout the history of the Christian Church. It is a terrible and sad story indeed. That history stands as a stumbling block to most Jewish people in even trying to hear the Christian message.

Through it all, God has remained faithful to his everlasting covenant, and His promises of future blessing are still awaiting God's people!

Chapter 18
ZIONISM

"*Zionism is racism*" announced the United Nations conference in 2000 AD in Durban, South Africa.

People today have a great deal of misunderstanding about the term and its meaning. A "Zionist" is one who believes that the Jewish people have a right to return to their promised Land of Israel!

The word "Zion" is used over 150 times in the Bible and refers to the Land of Israel, the city of Jerusalem, the children of Israel, the mountain of the LORD, the message of salvation which the Messiah of Israel will bring, the return of the Jewish people to their God-given Land, and even refers to the eternal home of all believers (Hebrews 12:22-23). Though some have called "Zionism" — "racism" — that is totally false! The word "Zion" is a great word, and even the LORD GOD of Israel is a "Zionist" — the One Who roars as a Lion out of Zion, which is clearly identified as the city of Jerusalem where God has put His Name

forever! Zion is the name given to God's people whom He has engraved on the palms of His hands (Isaiah 49:13-16).

Zechariah 9:9 is a wonderful prophecy referring to the coming of the Messiah into Jerusalem, riding on a donkey, lowly, humble, but having salvation! Zion is referring to the hope of eternal life and we must never forget that the Redeemer comes out of Zion, bringing salvation and His reward!

WHAT IS ZIONISM?

What Israel's Enemies Say:

1. Zionism is racism!
2. Zionism is apartheid!
3. Zionism is a Jewish conspiracy!
4. Zionism is a Jewish occupation of Arab land!

What The Bible Says:

The word *"Zion"* is used over 150 times in the Bible, and refers to the city of Jerusalem, the nation of Israel as a whole, to believers in the Messiah as the hope of Israel, to the Hill of Ophel, the original city of David, to one of the mountains upon which Jerusalem sits — Mount Zion — and to one of the gates of the city of Jerusalem — Zion's Gate (southwest side of the city).

ZION IS THE **PROPERTY** ON PLANET EARTH CALLED JERUSALEM AND ISRAEL!

Jerusalem is the most important city in the world and the eternal capital of the Nation of Israel.

Psalm 48:1-2 calls it *"the city of the great King"* and v. 8 adds *"the city of our God"* — cf. Psalm 147:12.

Isaiah 52:1 says that *"Zion"* is *"Jerusalem, the holy city."*

Isaiah 60:14 — *"The city of the LORD, the Zion of the Holy One of Israel."* cf. Isaiah 2:1-3; 33:20; 37:32

It refers to the land of Israel — Joel 2:1, 15

ZION IS THE **PEOPLE** THAT HAVE BEEN GRAVEN ON THE HANDS OF THE LORD!

Isaiah 49:13-16:

"Sing, O heavens; and be joyful, O earth; and break forth into singing, O mountains: for the LORD hath comforted His people and will have mercy upon His afflicted. But Zion said, The LORD hath forsaken me, and my Lord hath forgotten me. Can a woman forget her sucking child, that she should not have compassion on the son of her womb? Yea, they may forget, yet will I not forget thee."

Isaiah 62:11-12:

"Behold, the LORD hath proclaimed unto the end of the world, Say ye to the daughter of Zion,

Behold, thy salvation cometh; behold, His reward is with Him, and His work before Him. And they shall call them, The holy people, The redeemed of the LORD: and thou shalt be called, Sought out, A city not forsaken."

Joel 2:23:

"Be glad then, ye children of Zion, and rejoice in the LORD your God…"

Psalm 149:2:

"Let Israel rejoice in Him that made him: let the children of Zion be joyful in their King."

ZIONISM IS THE **PLAN** OF GOD TO RETURN HIS PEOPLE TO THE LAND OF ISRAEL!

Isaiah 43:5-7:

"Fear not: for I am with thee: I will bring thy seed from the east, and gather thee from the west; I will say to the north, Give up; and to the south, Keep not back: bring my sons from far, and my daughters from the ends of the earth; Even every one that is called by My Name: for I have created him for My glory, I have formed him; yea, I have made him."

Isaiah 51:11:

"Therefore the redeemed of the LORD shall

return, and come with singing unto Zion; and everlasting joy shall be upon their head: they shall obtain gladness and joy; and sorrow and mourning shall flee away."

ZION IS THE **PLACE** WHERE THE LORD DWELLS!

Psalm 9:11:

"Sing praise to the LORD, which dwelleth in Zion: declare among the people His doings."

Psalm 76:1-2:

"In Judah God is known: His Name is great in Israel. In Salem also is His tabernacle, and His dwelling place in Zion."

Psalm 135:21:

"Blessed be the LORD out of Zion, which dwelleth at Jerusalem. Praise ye the LORD."

Joel 3:16-17:

"The LORD also shall roar out of Zion, and utter His voice from Jerusalem; and the heavens and the earth shall shake: but the LORD will be the hope of His people, and the strength of the children of Israel. So shall ye know that I am the LORD your God dwelling in Zion, My holy mountain; then

shall Jerusalem be holy, and there shall no strangers pass through her any more."

Joel 3:21b:

"for the LORD dwelleth in Zion."

ZIONISM IS THE **PROCLAMATION** OF GOOD TIDINGS THAT ANNOUNCES THE COMING OF THE LORD GOD OF ISRAEL!

Isaiah 40:9-11:

"O Zion, that bringest good tidings, get thee up into the high mountain; O Jerusalem, that bringest good tidings, lift up thy voice with strength; lift it up, be not afraid; say unto the cities of Judah, Behold your God! Behold, the Lord GOD will come with strong hand, and His arm shall rule for Him; Behold, His reward is with Him, and His work before Him."

ZIONISM IS THE **PROPHECY** OF SALVATION THROUGH THE MESSIAH OF ISRAEL!

Isaiah 46:13b:

"and I will place salvation in Zion for Israel My glory."

Isaiah 62:11:

"Behold, the LORD hath proclaimed unto the

end of the world, Say ye to the daughter of Zion,
Behold, thy salvation cometh; behold, His reward
is with Him, and His work before Him."

Joel 2:32:

"And it shall come to pass, that whosoever shall call
on the Name of the LORD shall be delivered: for
in mount Zion and in Jerusalem shall be deliverance, as the LORD hath said, and in the remnant
whom the LORD shall call."

Zechariah 9:9:

"Rejoice greatly, O daughter of Zion; shout, O
daughter of Jerusalem; behold, thy King cometh
unto thee: He is just, and having salvation; lowly,
and riding upon an ass, and upon a colt the foal
of an ass."

ZION IS THE **_PROMISE_** OF OUR ETERNAL
HOME!

Hebrews 12:22-24:

"But ye are come unto mount Zion, and unto the
city of the living God, the heavenly Jerusalem,
and to an innumerable company of angels, to the
general assembly and church of the firstborn, which
are written in heaven, and to God the Judge of all,
and to the spirits of just men made perfect, and

to Jesus the Mediator of the new covenant, and to the blood of sprinkling, that speaketh better things than that of Abel."

Yes, ZIONISM is a Biblical name that should ring bells of joy in the heart of every true believer!

Chapter 19
1948 AD

In May 1948, Israel became an independent state after she was recognized by the United Nations as a country in her own right within the Middle East. If relations in pre-war Palestine had been fraught with difficulties, these difficulties paled into insignificance after Israel became a state in its own right.

Immediately on being granted its independence, Israel was attacked by a number of Arab nations. If Israel had faltered at this first hurdle, she would have ceased to exist as a state regardless of what the United Nations had decreed.

Before World War Two, Haganah had been, from the British viewpoint, a terrorist organization that used violence to defend the Jewish Agency. Haganah attacked Palestinian Arabs and aspects of British rule in Palestine.

By the time Israel had gained its independence, Haganah was effectively the army for Israel.

Many members of Haganah had gained military experience during World War II — ironically fighting for the same British military that they had been attacking before the war.

Israel was attacked on the same day it gained its independence — May 14th. The armies of Egypt, Lebanon, Syria and Iraq attacked Israel. With such a combined force attacking Israel, few would have given the new country any chance of survival.

In fact, Israel had internal problems as well as what was happening on its borders. The regular army had to be used to disband Irgun and the Stern Gang. Both of these had been classed as terrorist organizations by the British in pre-war Palestine.

David Ben-Gurion, Prime Minister and Defense Minister wanted the Israeli army to remain non-political and by using a combination of diplomacy and force, he removed these groups as a threat. The leaders of both groups were arrested but some members did join the army. At the height of the 1948 War, Israel's army numbered 100,000.

Though the attack on Israel was a surprising one, Israel was well equipped at a military level. The country had a Navy, and many in her army were experienced in combat as a result of World War II. Israel had also bought three B-17 bombers in America on the black market. In July 1948, these were used to attack the Egyptian capital, Cairo.

The Arab nations that attacked Israel faced one major problem. There was nothing to co-ordinate their attacks.

Each essentially attacked as a separate unit rather than as a combined force. However, the Israeli Army was under one single command structure and this proved to be very important. Israeli victories came on all the war fronts.

The Arab nations involved negotiated their own peace talks — a further sign that they were only united by their desire to attack Israel. Egypt signed a peace settlement in February 1949, and over the next few months Lebanon, Jordan and Syria did the same culminating in peace in July 1949. Iraq simply withdrew her forces but did not sign any peace settlement.

As a result of their military victory, Israel was able to expand the territory given to the State by the United Nations. However, this could only be at the expense of the Arab population that lived in these areas.

In the summer of 1949 there was no obvious leader in the Arab world who could head a campaign by the Arabs. Egypt seemed the most likely leader if only because of her size. However, the Egyptian Royal Family was far from popular and it was in this setting that Nasser rose to power. The scene was set for almost perpetual conflict between the Arab nations and Israel that culminated in the 1956, 1967 and 1973 wars.

The 1948 war, which the Israelis referred to as the "War of Independence", claimed 6,000 Israeli lives — but this was only 1% of the nation's population. The boost this victory gave to the Israelis was huge and put into perspective the 6,000 lives lost.

Ironically, those nations that had attacked Israel in May 1948, only lost slightly more men — 7,000. However, the damage to their morale was considerable.

BACKGROUND TO 1948 AD

After the Second World War, the British Mandate of Palestine came to an end. The surrounding Arab nations were also emerging from colonial rule. Transjordan, under the Hashemite ruler Abdullah I, gained independence from Britain in 1946 and was called Jordan, but it remained under heavy British influence. Egypt, while nominally independent, signed the Anglo-Egyptian Treaty of 1936 that included provisions by which Britain would maintain a garrison of troops on the Suez Canal. From 1945 on, Egypt attempted to renegotiate the terms of this treaty, which was viewed as a humiliating vestige of colonialism.

Lebanon became an independent state in 1943, but French troops would not withdraw until 1946, the same year that Syria won its independence from France.

In 1945, at British prompting, Egypt, Iraq, Lebanon, Saudi Arabia, Syria, Transjordan, and Yemen formed the Arab League to coordinate policy between the Arab states. Iraq and Transjordan coordinated policies closely, signing a mutual defense treaty, while Egypt, Syria, Lebanon, and Saudi Arabia feared that Transjordan would annex part or all of Palestine, and use it as a basis to attack or undermine Syria, Lebanon, and the Hejaz.

On 29 November 1947, the United Nations General Assembly approved a plan to resolve the Arab-Jewish conflict by partitioning Palestine into two states, one Jewish and one Arab.

Each state would comprise three major sections, linked by extraterritorial crossroads; the Arab state would also have an enclave at Jaffa. With about 32% of the population, the Jews would get 56% of the land, an area that contained 499,000 Jews and 438,000 Arabs, though most of this territory was in the inhospitable Negev Desert in the south. The Palestinian Arabs would get 42% of the land, which had a population of 818,000 Palestinian Arabs and 10,000 Jews.

In consideration of its religious significance, the Jerusalem area, including Bethlehem, with 100,000 Jews and an equal number of Palestinian Arabs, was to become a *Corpus Separatum*, to be administered by the UN.

The Jewish leadership accepted the partition plan as "the indispensable minimum," glad to gain international recognition but sorry that they did not receive more.

Arguing that the partition plan was unfair to the Arabs with regard to the population balance at that time, the representatives of the Palestinian Arabs and the Arab League firmly opposed the UN action and even rejected its authority to involve itself in the entire matter. They upheld "that the rule of Palestine should revert to its inhabitants, in accordance with the provisions of the Charter of the United Nations." According to Article 73b of the Charter, the UN should develop self-government of the peoples in a territory under its administration.

In the immediate aftermath of the United Nations' approval of the Partition plan, the explosions of joy amongst the Jewish community were counterbalanced by the expressions of discontent amongst the Arab community.

Soon thereafter, violence broke out and became more prevalent. Murders, reprisals, and counter-reprisals killed dozens on both sides.

In December 1947 and January 1948 an estimated nearly 1000 people were killed and 2000 injured. By the end of March, the figure had risen to 2,000 dead and 4,000 wounded. These figures correspond to an average of more than 100 deaths and 200 casualties per week in a population of 2,000,000.

Jewish soldiers took up positions at Mishmar Ha'emek, a settlement whose defenders repulsed repeated Arab attacks and inflicted a significant defeat on the Arab Liberation Army. From January onwards, operations became more militaristic, with the intervention into Palestine of a number of Arab Liberation Army regiments which divided up around the different coastal towns and reinforced Galilee and Samaria. Abd al-Qadir al-Husayni came from Egypt with several hundred men of the Army of the Holy War. At the time, military assessments were that the Palestinian Arabs were incapable of beating the Zionists.

Having recruited a few thousand volunteers, al-Husayni organized the blockade of the 100,000 Jewish residents of Jerusalem.

To counter this, the Yishuv authorities tried to supply the city with convoys of up to 100 armored vehicles, but the operation became more and more impractical, and more and more died in the process. By March, Al-Hussayni's tactic paid off. Almost all of Haganah's armored vehicles had been destroyed, the blockade remained in full operation, and hundreds of Haganah members who tried to bring supplies to the city had been killed. The situation for those in the Jewish settlements in the highly isolated Negev and northern Galilee was even more critical.

Since the Jewish population was under strict orders to hold their dominions at all costs, the insecurity across the country affected the Arab population more visibly. Up to 100,000 Palestinian Arabs, chiefly those from the upper classes, left the country to seek refuge abroad or in Samaria.

This situation caused the U.S. to retract its support for the partition plan, thus encouraging the Arab League to believe that the Palestinian Arabs, reinforced by the Arab Liberation Army, could put an end to the partition plan. The British, on the other hand, decided on 7 February 1948 to support the annexation of the Arab part of Palestine by Jordan.

Although a certain level of doubt took hold amongst Yishuv supporters, their apparent defeats were caused more by their wait-and-see policy than by weakness.

Ben-Gurion reorganized the Haganah and made conscription obligatory. Every Jewish man and woman in the country had to receive military training. Funds were gathered by Golda Meir from sympathizers in the United States, and Joseph Stalin supported the Zionist cause at the time, so Jewish representatives of Palestine were able to sign very important armament contracts in the East.

Other Haganah agents retrieved stockpiles from World War II, which helped equip the army further.

Operation Balak allowed arms and other equipment to be transported for the first time by the end of March.

Ben-Gurion assigned Yigael Yadin the responsibility to come up with a plan in preparation for the announced intervention of the Arab states. The result of his analysis was Plan Dalet, which was put in place from the beginning of April onwards. The adoption of Plan Dalet marked the second stage of the war, in which Haganah passed from the defensive to the offensive.

The first operation, named Operation Nachshon, consisted of lifting the blockade on Jerusalem. Fifteen hundred men from the Haganah's Givati Brigade and the Palmach's Harel brigade went about clearing the route to the city between 5 and 20 April.

Kastel dominated the Jerusalem approaches and its capture by Israeli forces during Operation Nachshon was a crucial turning point in the battle for the city.

The operation was successful, and enough foodstuffs to last two months were shipped to Jerusalem and distributed among the Jewish population. The success of the operation was added to by the death of al-Hussayni in combat. During this time, and beyond the command of Haganah or the framework of Plan Dalet, troops from Irgun and Lehi massacred more than 100 Arabs, mostly civilians, at Deir Yassin, a move that had an important impact on the Palestinian Arab population, and one that was criticized and lamented by all the principal Jewish authorities of the day.

At the same time, the first large-scale operation of the Arab Liberation Army ended in a debacle, with it being

roundly defeated at Mishmar Ha'emek and losing its Druze allies through defection.

Within the framework for the expansion of Jewish territory foreseen by Plan Dalet, the forces of Haganah, Palmach, and Irgun intended to conquer mixed zones. Tiberias, Haifa, Safed, Beisan, Jaffa, and Acre fell, resulting in the flight of more than 250,000 Palestinian Arabs.

The British had essentially withdrawn their troops. The situation pushed the leaders of the neighboring Arab states to intervene, but their preparation was not finalized, and they could not assemble forces capable of turning the tide of the war. The majority of Palestinian Arab hopes lay with the Arab Legion of Jordan's monarch, Abdullah I, but he had no intention of creating a Palestinian Arab-run state, instead hoping to annex as much of the territory of the British Mandate of Palestine as he could. He was playing a double game, being just as much in contact with the Jewish authorities as with the Arab League.

In preparation for the offensive, Haganah successfully launched Operation Yiftah to secure the Jewish settlements of Galilee, and Operation Kilshon, which created a united front around Jerusalem.

Golda Meir and Abdullah I met on 10 May to discuss the situation, but the meeting was inconclusive and their former agreements were not confirmed. On 13 May, the Arab Legion, backed by irregulars, attacked and took Kfar

Etzion, killing 127 of the 131 Jewish defenders and massacring the prisoners.

On 14 May 1948, David Ben-Gurion declared the independence of the State of Israel, and the war entered its second phase, with the intervention of several Arab states' armies the following day.

The War of Independence in 1948 AD was an amazing military victory, but those who fought in that war would tell you that it was the intervention and power of the LORD GOD of Israel that brought the victory.

Isaiah 66:8-10 says:

> *"Who hath heard such a thing? Who hath seen such things? Shall the earth be made to bring forth in one day? Or shall a nation be born at once? For as soon as Zion travailed, she brought forth her children. Shall I bring to the birth, and not cause to bring forth? saith the LORD: shall I cause to bring forth, and shut the womb? saith thy God. Rejoice ye with Jerusalem, and be glad with her, all ye that love her: rejoice for joy with her, all ye that mourn for her."*

Chapter 20
PRESENT DAY

Israel has experienced some miraculous military victories against overwhelming odds. Military leaders have continually reminded its citizens that their cause is just and Biblical, and that the LORD GOD of Israel has been behind these victories.

But, Israel should never presume upon the grace of the LORD. He is also a God of justice and judgment.

These past victories do not give Israel the right to do whatever they want, regardless of the consequences.

On September 13, 1993, the newspapers of the world carried the headlines in giant bold black lettering — *PEACE AT LAST!* The picture on the front pages of these newspapers showed former US President Bill Clinton standing between the late Yitzhak Rabin and the late Yassir Arafat as they were shaking hands, supposedly confirming publicly that a peace agreement had been reached.

What has followed for over the past 17 years has been nothing close to peace but rather constant violence and attacks. It is not Israel that has provoked the attacks; they are simply defending themselves and their citizens.

Is this really a Jew vs. Arab problem that is rooted deeply within the history of both groups? Many seem to argue that this is in fact the case. But, upon closer scrutiny of the situation, it is much more than just Arab resentment and hostility. One cannot possibly understand the circumstances without coming to grips with the beliefs and teachings of Islam, now claiming over one billion people under their control. Are all Arabs committed to Islam?

The answer is "NO!" Many Arabs are Christian in background and belief. Many of the so-called Arab regimes that dominate the landscape of the Middle East are not really "Arab" at all! Many Arabs may live within their borders, but they are treated poorly by Muslim dictators who use them as "pawns" in their resistance to the State of Israel.

IRAN — NOT Arab — formerly called Persia and traces its ancestors to Elam, a blood relative to the line of Abraham himself!

IRAQ — NOT Arab — the descendants of ancient Assyria and Babylon!

JORDAN — NOT Arab — descendants of Moab, Ammon, and Edom!

Chapter 20: PRESENT DAY

EGYPT — NOT Arab — descendants of Mizraim, from the line of Ham!

SAUDI ARABIA — NOT Arab — they are descendants of Sheba and Dedan, grandchildren of Abraham's wife, Keturah, whom he married after the death of Sarah.

The Arab peoples of the world are direct descendants from the 12 sons of Ishmael. **Then, what ties these nations together? The answer is ISLAM!**

Mohammed was a descendant of Ishmael's second son, Kedar. It is the Muslim religion that is the problem of the Middle East. They are at war with Jews and Christians as well. It is a religion of hatred and violence. Muslim warriors have often slaughtered each other throughout the history of Islam from the 7th century AD.

Israel must deal with terrorist groups like no other nation has to do.

The following are just a few of the groups that Israel faces today. Some are new and unknown, but are working to hurt Israel and its citizens.

- AL QAEDA
- HAMAS
- FATAH
- HIZBULLAH
- ISLAMIC JIHAD
- AL AQSA MARTYRS BRIGADE
- MUSLIM BROTHERHOOD

In addition to these groups, we have the Palestinian Authority (a product of Fatah) led by Mahmoud Abbas (also called Abu Mazen), who founded Fatah along with the late Yassir Arafat. Abbas wrote his doctorate at the University of Moscow on the premise that there was no holocaust in which six million Jews were slaughtered.

He continues to demand things that he has no right to say or expect. He says that he will "never make peace with Israel," which makes us all wonder why millions of dollars are being spent trying to accomplish a "false peace"?

Israel must also deal with a "nuclear" Middle East. Iran is a serious problem as it continues to develop its nuclear program. Others in the Middle East are also trying to go "nuclear." North Korea is also a problem as they are producing weapons of mass destruction that they are selling to the enemies of the State of Israel.

The United Nations continues to criticize and condemn the actions of Israel. Israel cannot be a member of the Security Council, and they are condemned by UN resolutions more than any other nation!

The talk about having two states living side by side in full security is a fantasy created by politicians who really do not see what Israel has to face every day!

The United Nations argued this possibility in the beginning when Israel declared its independence. The realities of the Holy Land, its boundaries and borders, and

its pressures are rarely understood by those who do not live there, or care to find out the truth!

Israel is NOT sending rockets and missiles into Palestinian Authority areas or into Gaza (which is controlled by Hamas) or into Lebanon at its northern border where Hizbullah has entrenched itself; That response is always in retaliation to what Israel's enemies have done. Israel does NOT shoot first! But, Israel must respond to what comes their way — thousands of rockets and missiles threaten Israel's citizens!

Psalm 94:1-14 could have been written in our present time. It says what the people of Israel experience on a daily basis and wonder how long the LORD will let this continue.

> *"O LORD God, to Whom vengeance belongeth; O God, to Whom vengeance belongeth, shew Thyself. Lift up Thyself, Thou Judge of the earth: render a reward to the proud. LORD, how long shall the wicked, how long shall the wicked triumph? How long shall they utter and speak hard things? And all the workers of iniquity boast themselves? They break in pieces Thy people, O LORD, and afflict thine heritage. They slay the widow and the stranger, and murder the fatherless. Yet they say, The LORD shall not see, neither shall the God of Jacob regard it. Understand, ye brutish among*

the people: and ye fools, when will ye be wise? He that planted the ear, shall He not hear? He that formed the eye, shall He not see? He that chastiseth the heathen, shall not He correct? He that teacheth man knowledge, shall not He know? The LORD knoweth the thoughts of man, that they are vanity. Blessed is the man whom Thou chastenest, O LORD, and teachest him out of Thy law; That Thou mayest give him rest from the days of adversity, until the pit be digged for the wicked. For the LORD will not cast off His people, neither will He forsake His inheritance."

Yes, the Judge of all the earth sees and hears it all, and one day all will be settled by Him, and peace at last will come with the return of the Messiah, our blessed Lord Yeshua!

The "present day" is filled with many challenges, threats, attacks, disappointments, and condemnation; but, God has NOT cast away His people or forgotten them; His covenant is everlasting and is not based on the merits or performance of His people — it is based on God's faithfulness, His foreknowledge, and His amazing forgiveness!

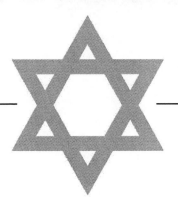

Part III

THE PROPHECIES ABOUT ISRAEL

"Remember the former things of old: for I am God, and there is none else; I am God, and there is none like Me, declaring the end from the beginning, and from ancient times the things that are not yet done, saying, My counsel shall stand, and I will do all My pleasure."

Isaiah 46:9-10

Chapter 21
THE RETURN

Before events happen in history, the LORD GOD of Israel predicts the details with amazing precision and accuracy. These promises of God are going to take place! Many of the prophecies of the Bible that were given hundreds of years before they happened have already taken place! Fulfilled prophecy is one of the outstanding characteristics of the Bible's inerrancy and inspiration.

A PROMISE OF <u>RETURN</u>

Isaiah 43:5-6 — *"Fear not: for I am with thee: I will bring thy seed from the east, and gather thee from the west; I will say to the north, Give up; and to the south, Keep not back: bring My sons from far, and My daughters from the ends of the earth."*

Ezekiel 36:24 — *"For I will take you from among the heathen, and gather you out of all countries, and will bring you into your own land."*

> Isaiah 35:10 — *"And the ransomed of the LORD shall return, and come to Zion with songs and everlasting joy upon their heads: they shall obtain joy and gladness, and sorrow and sighing shall flee away."*

There are already Jews living in Israel from over 180 countries of the world.

Some Bible teachers do not believe that the return of Jews to the promised Land today is the partial fulfillment of God's promise. The reason? They speak of Israel being in unbelief. But, do they not come back in unbelief (meaning faith in the Messiah) if the Holy Spirit is poured out upon the inhabitants of Jerusalem after they return? That's what Ezekiel 39:29 and Zechariah 12:10 argue.

While there are many secular Jews living in Israel as well as in other parts of the world, it is hardly a fair analysis to call them "unbelievers." The Hebrew Bible is still the basic textbook for Israel's children. Many are "Messianic" although they do not believe that Yeshua (Jesus) is the Messiah. They are aware of many prophecies about a coming Messiah and many Israelis believe that a Messiah is soon to appear, and that He is their only hope for peace.

What many Christians believe is that because the majority of those in Israel do not believe that Yeshua is the Messiah, this prevents them from believing that the return (Aliyah) is a fulfillment of Bible prophecy.

There are at least 10,000 Jews in Israel who do believe that Yeshua is the Messiah, and there are over 100 fellowships of believers who meet regularly to worship and praise our wonderful Lord. It is a small number but a significant one.

When the Holy Spirit is poured out on the Nation of Israel and salvation comes to Zion through the return of the Messiah, it appears from Zechariah 13:8-9, that only one-third of the people will put their faith and trust in Him.

Our conclusion is that the return of Jewish people to the promised Land that began in the late 19th century AD and continued throughout the 20th century AD into the 21st century AD is a partial fulfillment of the promise of God.

Close to seven million Jews now occupy the promised Land — it belongs to them by Divine command and covenant. But, there is still more involved in the promises about their return!

A PROMISE OF <u>RESURRECTION</u>

Ezekiel 37:11-14 — *"Then He said unto me, Son of man, these bones are the whole house of Israel. Behold, they say, 'Our bones are dried, and our hope is lost; we are cut off for our parts.' Therefore*

prophesy and say unto them, Thus saith the Lord GOD: Behold, O My people, I will open your graves, and cause you to come up out of your graves, and bring you into the land of Israel. And ye shall know that I am the LORD, when I have opened your graves, O My people, and brought you up out of your graves, and shall put My spirit in you, and ye shall live, and I shall place you in your own land: Then shall ye know that I the LORD have spoken it, and performed it, saith the LORD."

This famous passage refers to the *"whole house of Israel."* It appears to be speaking of the resurrection of the nation, not simply the promised resurrection of all believers (Jew and Gentile).

The promise clearly says that God will *"cause you to come up out of your graves and bring you into the LAND of Israel."*

For almost 2000 years, the Nation of Israel was non-existent. There have always been Jews living in the land that was called "Palestine." That name was given to the land in the 2nd century AD by Emperor Hadrian of Rome after he put down the 2nd Jewish revolt. In order to offend the Jews he gave the land a name that reminded them of their ancient enemies — the Philistines.

Some Christian Bibles have maps in the back of them that include a map of the Holy Land at the time

of Jesus Christ. The headings say "PALESTINE at the time of Christ."

But, that is incorrect! According to Matthew 2:21, when Joseph and Mary return to Israel with the young child (out of Egypt), the Bible says *"And he arose, and took the young child and His mother, and came into the LAND OF ISRAEL."* Yes, it was called "ERETZ YISRAEL" or the "LAND OF ISRAEL" at the time of Yeshua. The official name of the Nation today is "THE LAND OF ISRAEL."

For 400 hundred years Israel was under the control of the Ottoman Turks (broken in World War I) but they chose not to live there — Jews were still there.

Chapter 22
THE RESTORATION

The restoration of the Land of Israel is indeed a fulfillment of Bible prophecy. Before 1948 AD the land was desert sand, swamps, very few trees, and lots or rocks. No one cared anything about it, until the Jewish people started to return and were given international approval — starting with the Balfour declaration of 1917 AD which spoke of the Land as a "Jewish homeland."

The annihilation of six million Jews by the Nazi regime was used by God to bring them "home." It was not easy. Even Great Britain turned against them in spite of the Balfour declaration.

The 20th century AD was the beginning of the restoration, and although small at first, after the War of Independence, it was amazing to see what the Jewish people could accomplish!

The establishment of kibbutzim all over the Land was a key to its agricultural development. A kibbutz was like a

communal community of folks who pooled their resources and provided for each other in the process. Some of Israel's greatest leaders came from these humble beginnings (such as Moshe Dayan and Golda Meir). These efforts were foundational to the restoration, but the real source of growth came from the LORD God Himself.

A PROMISE OF <u>RESTORATION</u>

> Ezekiel 36:8 — *"But ye, O mountains of Israel, ye shall shoot forth your branches, and yield your fruit to My people of Israel, for they are at hand to come."*

Encouraged by the Jewish National Fund, millions of trees have been planted — all over the land, including in the desert!

> Ezekiel 36:30 — *"And I will multiply the fruit of the tree, and the increase of the field, that ye shall receive no more reproach of famine among the heathen."*

Israel has become a major supplier of fruit, exporting it around the world.

> Ezekiel 36:33-36 — *"Thus saith the Lord GOD: In the day that I shall have cleansed you from all your iniquities I will also cause you to dwell in the*

cities, and the wastes shall be builded. And the desolate land shall be tilled, whereas it lay desolate in the sight of all that passed by. And they shall say, 'This land, that was desolate is become like the Garden of Eden; and the waste and desolate and ruined cities are become fenced, and are inhabited." Then the heathen that are left round about you shall know that I the LORD build the ruined places, and plant that that was desolate: I the LORD have spoken it, and I will do it."

The productivity of the Negev (southern desert) is a marvel to behold. Consider the words of Isaiah 35:1-2:

"The wilderness and the solitary place shall be glad for them; and the desert shall rejoice, and blossom as the rose. It shall blossom abundantly, and rejoice even with joy and singing: the glory of Lebanon shall be given unto it, the excellency of Carmel and Sharon, they shall see the glory of the LORD, and the excellency of our God."

Isaiah 41:19-20
"I will plant in the wilderness the cedar, the shittah tree, and the myrtle, and the oil tree; I will set in the desert the fir tree, and the pine, and box tree together: That they may see, and know, and consider, and understand together, that the hand of

the LORD hath done this, and the Holy One of Israel hath created it."

Just for the record — all of these trees are growing in the desert today!

The restoration of the Land, the rebuilding of the "waste places" and the cities that now dot the landscape — all of this was predicted by God to take place in the future when He begins to wrap up human history with the coming of His Messiah, our blessed Lord Yeshua!

Chapter 23
JERUSALEM

When dealing with the prophecies relating to the Nation of Israel, one cannot help discussing the most important city in the world — JERUSALEM, the holy city.

Jerusalem is mentioned 811 times in the Bible; not once in the Quran. Muslims today want to include Jerusalem as their third most holy city after Mecca and Medina. But, before Israel came in 1948 there was no such teaching or concern.

It is called "Salem" on 4 occasions, including the first mention of it in Genesis 14:18. Psalm 76:1-2 says *"In Judah God is known; His Name is great in Israel. In Salem also is His tabernacle, and His dwelling place in Zion."*

The word "Zion" refers to Jerusalem 152 times. It is also called the "holy city" 10 times, and the "city of God" twice.

It is called "city of truth" — "the city of the great King" — "the city of Judah" and "the city of David."

Psalm 46:4 says *"There is a river, the streams whereof shall make glad the city of God, the holy place of the tabernacle of the Most High."*

Psalm 87:1-3 says *"His foundation is in the holy mountains. The LORD loveth the gates of Zion more than all the dwellings of Jacob. Glorious things are spoken of thee, Zion, city of God."*

Psalm 48:2 calls it *"the joy of the whole earth, ... the city of the great King."*

Psalm 137:6 refers to it as *"my chief joy."*

Psalm 87:2 says *"The Lord loveth the gates of Zion more than all the dwellings of Jacob."*

It is the place that the LORD God chose to put His name forever!

II Chronicles 6:6 says, *But I have chosen Jerusalem, that My Name might be there."*

In *Psalm 76:1-2* we read: *"In Judah is God known: His Name is great in Israel. In Salem also is His tabernacle, and His dwelling place in Zion."*

Psalm 99:2 says, *"The Lord is great in Zion; and He is high above all the people."*

Psalm 132:13-14 makes it very clear: *"For the Lord hath chosen Zion; He hath desired it for His habitation. This is My rest for ever; here will I dwell; for I have desired it."*

Psalm 135:21 adds, *"Blessed be the Lord out of <u>Zion</u>, which dwelleth at <u>Jerusalem</u>."*

THE PLACE WHERE ABRAHAM WAS BLESSED!

Genesis 14:18-19 says, *"Melchizedek king of <u>Salem</u> brought forth bread and wine: and he was the priest of the most high God. And he blessed him, and said, Blessed be Abram of the most high God, possessor of heaven and earth."* (Hebrews 7:1 confirms the story.)

THE PLACE FOR THE TEMPLE

II Samuel 5:4-9 — Verse 7 says *"Nevertheless David took the stronghold of <u>Zion</u>; the same is the <u>city of David</u>."*

In II Samuel 24:18-25 we learn that David purchased the site of the present Temple Mount from Aravnah the Jebusite and built an altar there.

II Chronicles 3:1 says, *"Then Solomon began to build the house of the Lord at <u>Jerusalem</u> in mount Moriyah…in the place that David had prepared in the threshing-floor of Ornan the Jebusite."*

The Lord appeared to Solomon and said in II Chronicles 7:16 — *"For now I have chosen and sanctified this house, that My Name may be there forever; and Mine eyes and Mine heart shall be there perpetually."*

THE PROPHECY OF THE DESTRUCTION OF JERUSALEM

Luke 21:20 states, *"And when ye shall see Jerusalem compassed with armies, then know that the desolation is nigh."*

Verse 24 says *"Jerusalem shall be trodden down of the Gentiles, until the times of the Gentiles be fulfilled."*

The knowledge of this terrible destruction of the city caused our Lord to weep over the city. Luke 19:41 says *"And when He was come near, He beheld the city, and wept over it."*

NOTE: The destruction of Jerusalem by Babylon in 586 BC and by Rome in 70 AD — both happened on the 9th of AV (day of fasting).

FUTURE PROPHECIES OF THE CITY OF JERUSALEM

Zechariah 12:2-3 says, *"Behold, I will make Jerusalem a cup of trembling unto all the people round about"* and *"And in that day will I make Jerusalem a burdensome stone for all people."*

Revelation 11:1-2 *states, "And there was given me a reed like unto a rod: and the angel stood, saying, Rise, and measure the temple of God, and the altar, and them that worship therein. But the court which is without the temple leave out, and measure it not; for it is given unto the Gentiles: and the holy city shall they tread under foot forty and two months."*

Zechariah 12:9 says, *"And it shall come to pass in that day, that I will seek to destroy all the nations that come against Jerusalem."*

Zechariah 14:2 says, *"For I will gather all nations against Jerusalem to battle"*

Zechariah 12:10 states, *"And I will pour upon the house of David, and upon the inhabitants of Jerusalem, the Spirit of grace and of supplications; and they shall look upon Me Whom they have pierced…"*

Zechariah 13:1 — *"In that day there shall be a fountain opened to the house of David and to the inhabitants of Jerusalem for sin and for uncleanness."*

Joel 2:32 says, *"And it shall come to pass, that whosoever shall call on the Name of the Lord shall be delivered: for in mount Zion and in Jerusalem shall be deliverance…"*

Isaiah 62:11 — *"Behold, the LORD hath proclaimed unto the end of the world, Say ye to the daughter of Zion, Behold thy salvation cometh; behold, His reward is with Him, and His work before Him"*

Zechariah 9:9 says, *"Rejoice greatly, O daughter of Zion; shout, O daughter of Jerusalem: behold, thy King cometh unto thee: He is just, and having salvation; lowly, and riding upon an ass, and upon a colt the foal of an ass."*

Isaiah 2:2-3 speaks of a future day: "*And it shall come to pass in the last days, that the mountain of the Lord's house shall be established in the top of the mountains, and shall be exalted above the hills; and all nations shall flow unto it....for out of <u>Zion</u> shall go forth the law, and the word of the Lord from <u>Jerusalem</u>.*"

Zechariah 14:16 says, "*And it shall come to pass, that every one that is left of all the nations which came against <u>Jerusalem</u> shall even go up from year to year to worship the King, the Lord of hosts...*"

JERUSALEM — the most important city in the world — the eternal capital of the Nation of Israel!

Chapter 24
THE TEMPLE

No discussion of future prophecies being fulfilled would be complete without describing the promises of God about a future temple — THE TEMPLE OF THE MESSIAH!

The interest in the rebuilding of the Jewish Temple has accelerated in recent days. The Jewish Sanhedrin has been reestablished and their efforts are centered in the reestablishment of the Jewish Temple.

The word "temple" is used 204 times in the Bible — 117 of those times in the NT. The words "temple of the Lord" are found 24 times, once in the NT. The words "temple of God" appear 9 times. The word "tabernacle" is used 328 times, 20 in the NT. The words "holy place" are found 60 times — 5 in the NT. The words "the most holy" appear 24 times and the words "the most holy place" another 10 times. The phrase "the mountain of the Lord" is found 4 times, and the words "the house of the Lord" occur 234

times. Other usages include *"the mount of the Lord"* and *"the holy mount."* The word *"sanctuary"* appears 137 times of which 21 usages are in the last nine chapters of Ezekiel that describe a future temple of the Messiah Himself. The evidence totals up to over 1,000 usages in the Bible. Isaiah 27:13 speaks of a future day when people will come to *"worship the Lord in the holy mount at Jerusalem."*

The Hebrew word for *"temple"* that is used 81 times is the word *"hekal"* — meaning *"big house."* However, in describing the temple, the Bible uses the term *"Beit Adonai"* meaning *"the house of the Lord"* or *"Beit Elohim"* — *"the house of God."* Both the tabernacle and the temple are referred to with the Hebrew word *"mishkan"* meaning *"dwelling."*

The words *"Beit Hamikdash"* meaning *"the house of holiness"* are translated *"sanctuary"* and today describe the temple.

In spite of many attempts by the Islamic world to deny the presence of a Jewish temple on the holy mount in Jerusalem, the evidence speaks powerfully that they are wrong. A discovery from the caves where the Dead Sea Scrolls were found has produced nine rare silver coins that date back to the Jewish revolt in the 2nd century AD. The largest Jewish coin ever issued, a half-ounce silver coin called the "Petra Drachma" has been found. One side of the coin shows Jerusalem's Second Temple which

was destroyed by the Romans in 70 AD. The other side of the coin shows the image of the four plants known as the four species used during ceremonies of the Feast of Sukkot or Tabernacles.

HOW MANY TEMPLES?

While most Biblical scholars refer to three temples (Solomon, Herod, and Messiah) the words describing the temple are used in the Bible in the following ways:

The Tabernacle of Moses

Exodus 25:8 says, *"and let them make Me a <u>Sanctuary</u>; that I may dwell among them."*

The Temple of Solomon

II Chronicles 3:1 — This temple was destroyed in 586 BC by Babylon — II Chronicles 36:19 says, *"and they burnt the <u>house</u> of God, and brake down the wall of Jerusalem; and burnt all the palaces thereof with fire."*

The Restored Temple

It was built under the protection of Persia and the preaching of Haggai and Zechariah and the leadership of Zerubbabel and Joshua — Ezra 5:1-2.

Herod's Temple

This was the project of King Herod — usually referred to as the Second Temple — destroyed as Yeshua predicted in 70 AD — Matthew 24:1-2; Luke 21:20-24

The Tribulation Temple

This temple will exist during the coming Tribulation — Revelation 11:1-2 — the Bible seems to teach the following about this temple:

A political <u>AGREEMENT</u> will allow a place for Jewish worship on the Temple Mount, but its location will be shared — Daniel 9:27.

> Rev. 11:2 — *"But the court which is without the <u>temple</u> leave out, and measure it not; for it is given unto the Gentiles; and the holy city shall they tread under foot forty and two months."*

A personal <u>ARROGANCE</u> of a coming world leader will cause him to enter the temple and demand that he be worshipped — Daniel 11:36-37, 45; Matthew 24:15

> II Thessalonians 2:4 — *"so that he as God sitteth in the <u>temple</u> of God, shewing himself that he is God."*

The Messianic Temple

This is the one which Ezekiel saw in his vision recorded in chapters 40-48:

Ezekiel 41:1 — *"Afterward he brought me to the temple..."*

Ezekiel 43:4 — *"And the glory of the LORD came into the house..."* It is the same house to which Isaiah referred in Isaiah 2:3: *"Come ye, and let us go up to the mountain of the LORD, to the house of the God of Jacob..."*

Micah 4:1 — *"But in the last days it shall come to pass, that the mountain of the house of the LORD shall be established in the top of the mountains, and it shall be exalted above the hills; and people shall flow into it."*

It is called "The Temple of the Messiah" for Zechariah 6:12-13 prophesies *"Behold, the Man whose name is The Branch; and He shall grow up out of His place, and He shall build the temple of the LORD; Even He shall build the temple of the LORD; and He shall bear the glory, and shall sit and rule upon His throne; and He shall be a priest upon His throne..."*

There are numerous Bible teachers and scholars who do not believe that a literal Third Temple is going to be built by the Messiah. They believe that the Church is that temple.

The preparations and plans of the nation of Israel to build the temple are considered by certain scholars as insignificant and unrelated to the issue. The desires of the Jewish people around the world mean nothing to them for

in their view the Church has replaced Israel as the people of God and as the true temple of God.

The Jerusalem Talmud (*Yoma 1:1*) says: "*Each generation in which the Temple is not rebuilt is considered as if they destroyed the Temple.*"

Elwood McQuaid said in an article in the magazine *Israel My Glory*: "*I believe that the preparations for the rebuilding of the Temple today are extremely significant. I think we're seeing a time when in the hearts of people they're saying the time has come.*"

When Israel captured the Temple Mount in June of 1967, Defense Forces Chief Rabbi General Shlomo Goren said on that day:

> "*We have taken the city of God; we are entering the Messianic era for the Jewish people. We took an oath today, while capturing the city —on our blood we took an oath that we will never give it up — we will never leave this place. The Wailing Wall belongs to us. The holy place* (Temple Mount) *was our place first, and our God's place. From here we do not move — Never — NEVER!*"

Rabbi Chaim Richman of the Temple Mount Faithful has said:

> "*The Holy Temple was not just some magnificent building or synagogue rooted in Jerusalem's*

ancient Biblical past; it was an arena of cosmic themes, a place where man could meet with his Creator; it is the reality of the living memory of that relationship as it once was, and the dream of its renewal, as promised by God Himself, that keeps the fires of the Temple altar burning within the collective heart of the nation of Israel, and the hearts of all those who cherish Israel's God and His message for humanity."

Yes, there will be a Temple built by the Messiah Himself, and all nations will come to Jerusalem to worship the LORD, the KING!

Chapter 25
THE DAY OF THE LORD

One of the most amazing prophecies of the Bible deals with a coming period of time known as "THE DAY OF THE LORD." It is used 25 times in the Bible.

The Hebrew words *"yom Yahveh"* appear 21 times in the Jewish Bible, the Tanakh, the Old Testament. The New Testament records the words on four occasions *"he hemera Kuriou"* — In I Thessalonians 5:4, it refers to it with the simple words *"he hemera"* — *"the day"* — translated as *"that day."*

II Thessalonians 2:2 uses the term *"the day of Christ"* (Greek: *he hemera tou Christou*) but Bible teachers disagree on the meaning of this term as to whether it is referring to the Rapture of the Church or is it synonymous with the term *"the Day of the LORD"*?

Acts 2:17-21 uses the term *"that great and notable day of the Lord"* and is quoting the passage in Joel 2:28-32 which clearly speaks of *"the Day of the LORD."*

Luke 17:26-37 speaks of the *"day when the Son of Man is revealed* (v. 30)*."* We also have parallel passages in Matthew 24:15-22, 29, 36; 25:13; Mark 13:19, 24-32. We also read of the *"day of judgment"* in passages like Matthew 10:15; 11:22, 24; 12:36; Romans 2:5, 16; II Peter 3:7 and Jude 1:6. II Peter 3:12 speaks of the *"day of God"* and associates it with the term *"day of the LORD."* II Thessalonians 1:9-10 speaks of *"in that day."*

John 6:39-40 speaks of the *"last day"* when the resurrection will occur.

We also have the term *"the day of our Lord Jesus Christ"* or *"the day of Christ"* in I Corinthians 1:8; 3:13; II Corinthians 1:14.

Ephesians 4:30 refers to the *"day of redemption."*

In the Book of Revelation we have the term the *"great day of His wrath"* in 6:17 and the *"great day of God Almighty"* in 16:14 which refers in the context to the Battle of Armageddon.

Believers know that this *"day"* will come as a *"thief in the night."* It is also clear that it will be preceded by a call for *"peace and safety."* The reference to *"travail upon a woman with child"* connects it to the time of *"Jacob's trouble"* (Jeremiah 30:6-11) and the warnings of the Hebrew prophets about a terrible time of future tribulation and suffering. Isaiah 13:6-13 clearly connects the imagery of a woman travailing with the coming of the *"day of the LORD."*

It is a Day of <u>Deception!</u>

In I Thessalonians 5:3 it is clear that the world will be deceived by a call for *"peace and safety."* In a previous time of trouble, Israel was warned in Jeremiah 6:13-14 and 8:9-11 about so-called spiritual leaders who were *"given to covetousness"* and who were deceiving people by saying: *"Peace, peace; when there is no peace."*

Jeremiah 23:1-8 tells us that in the days of the coming of Messiah there will be real peace, but that the shepherds of Israel who deceived the people in the past will be replaced.

Ezekiel 13:1-16 speaks powerfully of the same problem of deception. The prophet warns of how religious leaders (he calls them *"foolish prophets"*) will *"follow their own spirit"* and in fact, they have *"seen nothing."* They have lied to the people about what God said and have *"spoken vanity."* Verse 10 says that they have *"seduced"* God's people by saying *"Peace; and there was no peace."*

It is a Day of <u>Darkness!</u>

Exodus 10:21-23 speaks of the awful darkness that fell upon the land of Egypt for three days. It described it as *"darkness which may be felt."* In describing what hell is like, the Bible uses the term *"outer darkness."* Joel 2:2 says of the coming *"day of the LORD"* that it is *"a day of darkness*

and of gloominess, a day of clouds and of thick darkness." He goes on to say that "there hath not been ever the like, neither shall be any more after it, even to the years of many generations." Amos 5:18-20 describes the "day of the LORD" in a similar manner: "the day of the LORD is darkness, and not light." Verse 20 adds: "Shall not the day of the LORD be darkness, and not light? Even very dark, and no brightness in it?" Zephaniah 1:15 says: "a day of darkness and gloominess, a day of clouds and thick darkness."

In Revelation 8:12 the Bible speaks of the fourth trumpet judgment with these words: "the third part of the sun was smitten, and the third part of the moon, and the third part of the stars; so as the third part of them was darkened, and the day shone not for a third part of it, and the night likewise." While the word "darkness" is often used in a symbolical sense of sin and unrighteousness (cf. I John 1:5-6; 2:9-11) the language concerning the coming "day of the LORD" speaks loudly of literal darkness. Interestingly, Revelation 21:25 says of the heavenly city "for there shall be no night there." That is repeated in Revelation 22:5.

One of the clear and consistent descriptions of this terrible period of time is the fact of what Joel 2:10 says: "the sun and the moon shall be dark, and the stars shall withdraw their shining."

Isaiah 13:10 speaks of this terrible darkness when it says "For the stars of heaven and the constellations thereof

shall not give their light: the sun shall be darkened in his going forth, and the moon shall not cause her light to shine."

Yeshua predicted in Matthew 24:29: *"Immediately after the tribulation of those days shall the sun be darkened, and the moon shall not give her light, and the stars shall fall from heaven, and the powers of the heavens shall be shaken."*

It is a Day of <u>Distress!</u>

It is obvious from the many passages describing this coming *"day of the LORD"* that panic will hit world leadership — people will not know what to do under the holocaust of terror that will come from God upon this planet! Joel 2:1 speaks of this when it says *"let all the inhabitants of the land tremble."* In Joel 2:11 we read: *"for the day of the LORD is great and very terrible; and who can abide it?"*

Zephaniah 1:15 says of the coming *"day of the LORD"* that it is a *"day of trouble and distress."* In verse 17 it adds: *"And I will bring distress upon men, that they shall walk like blind men, because they have sinned against the LORD: and their blood shall be poured out as dust, and their flesh as the dung."*

Isaiah 13:7-8 speaks graphically of the *"distress"* that will come: *"Therefore shall all hands be faint, and every man's heart shall melt: and they shall be afraid: pangs and sorrows shall take hold of them; they shall be in pain as a woman that*

travaileth: they shall be amazed one at another; their faces shall be as flames."

In Luke 21:25-26 our Lord Yeshua prophesied that *"upon the earth distress of nations, with perplexity; the sea and the waves roaring; men's hearts failing them for fear, and for looking after those things which are coming on the earth: for the powers of heaven shall be shaken."*

It is a Day of <u>Destruction!</u>

Isaiah 13:6 says: *"Howl ye; for the day of the LORD is at hand; it shall come as a destruction from the Almighty."* Verse 9 says: *"Behold, the day of the LORD cometh, cruel both with wrath and fierce anger, to lay the land desolate."* Verse 13 adds: *"Therefore I will shake the heavens, and the earth shall remove out of her place, in the wrath of the LORD of hosts, and in the day of His fierce anger."*

Joel 1:15 says: *"Alas for the day! For the day of the LORD is at hand, and as a destruction from the Almighty shall it come."*

I Thessalonians 5:3 says: *"For when they shall say, Peace and safety; then sudden destruction cometh upon them, as travail upon a woman with child; and they shall not escape."*

II Thessalonians 1:8-9 says of this future day: *"In flaming fire taking vengeance on them that know not God, and that obey not the gospel of our Lord Jesus Christ: Who*

shall be punished with everlasting destruction from the presence of the Lord, and from the glory of His power."

II Peter 3:10 teaches: *"But the day of the Lord will come as a thief in the night; in the which the heavens shall pass away with a great noise, and the elements shall melt with fervent heat, the earth also and the works that are therein shall be burned up."*

Revelation 16:20 says: *"And every island fled away, and the mountains were not found."*

Revelation 19:15 adds: *"And out of His mouth goeth a sharp sword, that with it He should smite the nations; and He shall rule them with a rod of iron: and He treadeth the winepress of the fierceness and wrath of Almighty God."*

It is a Day of <u>Death!</u>

Isaiah 13:9 says that this coming *"day of the LORD"* will *"destroy the sinners thereof out of it."* Verse 11 adds: *"And I will punish the world for their evil, and the wicked for their iniquity; and I will cause the arrogancy of the proud to cease, and will lay low the haughtiness of the terrible."*

Revelation 6:8: *"And power was given unto them over the fourth part of the earth, to kill with sword, and with hunger, and with death, and with the beasts of the earth."*

Revelation 8:11: *"and many men died of the waters, because they were made bitter."*

Revelation 9:15 speaks of the four angels who were loosed from their bondage in the river Euphrates and says: *"for to slay the third part of men."*

Revelation 9:20: *"And the rest of the men which were not killed by these plagues yet repented not of the works of their hands, that they should not worship devils, and idols of gold, and silver, and brass, and stone, and of wood; which neither can see, not hear, nor walk."*

Revelation 11:7 speaks about the two witnesses and says: *"And when they shall have finished their testimony, the beast that ascendeth out of the bottomless pit shall make war against them, and shall overcome them, and kill them."* And, in Revelation 13:7 this coming world leader will *"make war with the saints, and…overcome them."* Verse 15 says of the power of the false prophet: *"and cause that as many as would not worship the image of the beast should be killed."*

Revelation 20:4 refers to the following: *"And I saw the souls of them that were beheaded for the witness of Jesus, and for the word of God, and which had not worshipped the beast, neither his image, neither had received his mark upon their foreheads, or in their hands"*

It is a Day of <u>Deliverance!</u>

In spite of the terrible events and tragedies described in the Bible concerning the coming *"day of the LORD,"* there

is hope in the midst of it. Deliverance has been promised to some who experience this holocaust of terror that is coming to planet earth.

Joel 2:10-14 speaks of this deliverance: *"The earth shall quake before them; the heavens shall tremble: the sun and the moon shall be dark, and the stars shall withdraw their shining: And the LORD shall utter His voice before His army: for His camp is very great: for He is strong that executeth His word: for the day of the LORD is great and very terrible; and who can abide it? Therefore also now, saith the LORD, turn ye even to Me with all your heart, and with fasting, and with weeping, and with mourning: And rend your heart, and not your garments, and turn unto the LORD your God: for He is gracious and merciful, slow to anger, and of great kindness, and repenteth Him of the evil. Who knoweth if he will return and repent, and leave a blessing behind him; even a meat offering and a drink offering unto the LORD your God?"*

The message is clear — deliverance is promised to those who will *"turn"* to the Lord *"with all your heart."* Joel 2:28-32 is the third chapter of *Joel* in the Hebrew Bible. It speaks of the day when the LORD will *"pour out My Spirit upon all flesh."* Zechariah 12:10 says that the LORD will do this upon the *"inhabitants of Jerusalem"* — Israel will be back in the land once again, and God will deliver all who *"call on the Name of the LORD"* (Joel 2:32). Joel 3:16 says that *"the LORD will be the hope*

of His people, and the strength of the children of Israel." Joel 3:20 states clearly that *"Judah shall dwell forever, and Jerusalem from generation to generation."*

In Peter's message at Shavuot (Pentecost) in Acts 2:16-21 he quoted from Joel 2:28-32 and his message said *"And it shall come to pass that whosoever shall call on the Name of the Lord shall be saved."* That is God's promise — there is deliverance coming during the *"day of the LORD."*

What Should Be Our Response?

We should <u>REMEMBER</u> that we do not know the day or the hour when it will come! — Matthew 24:36

We should <u>REALIZE</u> the significance of a peace agreement between Israel and its enemies! — I Thessalonians 5:1-3

We should <u>RELY</u> upon the promises of God's deliverance for believers today! — I Thessalonians 5:9; Revelation 3:10

We should <u>RESPOND</u> by watchfulness, prayer, and readiness! — Matthew 24:42, 44; 25:13; Mark 13:33-37; Luke 21:36

We should <u>REPENT</u> of our sins and turn to the Lord before it is too late! — II Chronicles 7:14; Isaiah 55:6-7; Acts 3:19

Chapter 26
ARMAGEDDON

The movies and books available on this subject have convinced many people that an event similar to what the Bible describes as the final battle of all time — will indeed happen on planet earth! Nations in their desire for weapons of mass destruction and the ability to conquer others, are pursuing rapidly that which will bring us to a global conflict.

The term *"Armageddon"* is found in Revelation 16:12-16 and means *"the hill of Megiddo."*

It was the historic site of many ancient battles. Revelation 14:19-20 describes it as *"the great winepress of the wrath of God."* In that passage it speaks of the *"blood"* that comes out of the *"winepress"* rising to the level of the *"horse bridles,"* and the distance covered as being *"a thousand and six hundred furlongs."*

The Greek word is *stadia* and a *stadion* equals 600 ft., making a total of 960,000 ft. — divide by 5280 ft. (1 mile)

and you have a distance of 180 miles. There are various viewpoints concerning these facts:

+ It will be the future radius around Jerusalem.

+ It involves the length of the Jordanian valley.

+ It involves the distance from Megiddo to Bozrah, the capital of ancient Edom (Jordan).

+ It refers to the entire land of Israel — from north to south.

+ It is a term describing the final battle of all battles — the day when the LORD God brings His vengeance upon a world that has turned its back on Him.

Who Will be Involved in This Battle of Armageddon?

Revelation 16:14 says *"the whole world."*

Joel 3:11 says *"all ye heathen"* and v. 14 adds: *"Multitudes, multitudes in the valley of decision."*

Zechariah 12:3 says *"all the people of the earth"* — Verse 9 says *"all the nations"* — Zech. 14:2 quotes the LORD Himself saying *"I will gather all nations against Jerusalem to battle."*

It appears from the Biblical evidence that this is a global conflict involving all nations of the world, and that the specific attack will come against the Nation of Israel.

What Will Cause the World to be Afraid of This Event?

Matthew 24:29 says *"the sun shall be darkened and the moon shall not give her light, and the stars shall fall from heaven, and the powers of the heavens shall be shaken."*

Amos 5:18-20 calls it *"darkness and not light."*

Zephaniah 1:15 says that it will be *"a day of clouds and thick darkness."*

Joel 2:30-31 quotes the LORD as saying *"And I will shew wonders in the heavens and in the earth, blood, and fire, and pillars of smoke. The sun shall be turned into darkness, and the moon into blood, before the great and the terrible day of the LORD come."*

Luke 21:26 says *"Men's hearts failing them for fear, and for looking after those things which are coming on the earth."*

The nations of the world will know that there is a major PLAYER in this conflict that they have ignored for years!

How Will Israel Possibly Survive This Worldwide Attack?

Although Bible teachers disagree on the interpretation of the words of Yeshua in Matthew 24:32-35, we believe that He is describing the survival of Israel:

> *"Now learn a parable of the fig tree; When his branch is yet tender, and putteth forth leaves, ye know that summer is nigh; So likewise ye, when ye shall see all these things, know that it is near, even at the doors. Verily I say unto you, This generation shall not pass, till all these things be fulfilled. Heaven and earth shall pass away, but My words shall not pass away."*

The disagreements center in the interpretation of our Lord's words *"This generation shall not pass."*

Various viewpoints include the following:

His words refer to 40 years — Psalm 95:10; Heb. 3:9-10 — Israel was in the wilderness 40 years and was called *"that generation."*

It might refer to a man's life of 70-80 years — Psalm 90:10.

A major view of many Bible teachers is that our Lord's words are referring to those listening at the time — some of them would still be alive in 70 AD when Rome destroyed Jerusalem and its Temple. This view is the major view of

those who are "preterists" (Latin for "past") and believe that the predictions of our Lord in Matthew 24-25 refer to those living before and during 70 AD.

We believe that the correct view is that our Lord was referring to the Nation of Israel — Jeremiah 31:35-37 promises that *the Nation of Israel will never cease to exist.* The survival of Israel is certain, no matter how severe Armageddon is.

In the immediate context of Matthew 24, our Lord already referred to Israel in this way in Matthew 23:36 — *"Verily I say unto you, All these things shall come upon this generation."*

ISRAEL'S SURVIVAL IS GUARANTEED BY THE GOD WHO GAVE THEM AN EVERLASTING COVENANT!

Rom. 11:1-2a — *"God hath not cast away His people which He foreknew."*

God will be faithful to His covenant with Abraham, Isaac, and Jacob!

WHEN THE MESSIAH COMES AT ARMAGEDDON...
It is the day of the Lord's REVENGE!

Isaiah 63:4 — *"For the day of vengeance is in Mine heart, and the year of My redeemed is come."*

Ezekiel 38:19 — *"For in My jealousy and in the fire of My wrath have I spoken, Surely in that day there shall be a great shaking in the Land of Israel."*

Nahum 1:2 — *"God is jealous, and the LORD revengeth; the LORD revengeth, and is furious; the LORD will take vengeance on His adversaries, and He reserveth wrath for His enemies."*

It is the day of the Lord's <u>REVELATION</u> of Himself!

Ezekiel 38:23 — *"Thus will I magnify Myself, and sanctify Myself; and I will be known in the eyes of many nations, and they shall know that I am the LORD."*

Ezekiel 39:21-22 — *"And I will set My glory among the heathen (nations), and all the heathen shall see My judgment that I have executed, and My hand that I have laid upon them. So the house of Israel shall know that I am the LORD their God from that day and forward."*

Joel 3:16-17 — *"The LORD also shall roar out of Zion, and utter His voice from Jerusalem; and the heavens and the earth shall shake: but the LORD will be the hope of His people, and the strength of the children of Israel. So shall ye know that I am the LORD your God dwelling in Zion, My holy mountain; then shall Jerusalem be holy, and there shall no strangers pass through her anymore."*

It is the day of the Lord's <u>RENNOVATION</u> of the entire planet!

II Peter 3:10-13 — *"But the day of the LORD will come as a thief in the night; in the which the heavens shall pass away with a great noise, and the elements shall melt with fervent heat, the earth also and the works that are therein shall be burned up. Seeing then that all these things shall be dissolved, what manner of persons ought ye to be in all holy conversation and godliness, Looking for and hasting unto the coming of the day of God, wherein the heavens being on fire shall be dissolved, and the elements shall melt with fervent heat? Nevertheless we, according to His promise, look for new heavens and a new earth, wherein dwelleth righteousness."*

Some Bible teachers place this event after the Millennium (1000 year reign of Messiah), but that seems to distort the obvious point of the passage. This renovation follows the Tribulation, and sets up a world that describes the Messiah ruling and reigning.

WHY ARMAGEDDON?

In one sense, it is not for us to ask "Why?" Whatever the LORD has planned, He will do, and does not need our permission or understanding! But consider the following possibilities regarding the motivation of the LORD behind Armageddon:

The <u>PROBLEM</u> of Jerusalem
will be decided!

Zech. 12:1-3 — *"The burden of the word of the LORD for Israel, saith the LORD, which stretcheth forth the heavens, and layeth the foundation of the earth, and formeth the spirit of man within him. Behold, I will make Jerusalem a cup of trembling unto all the people round about, when they shall be in the siege both against Judah and against Jerusalem. And in that day will I make Jerusalem a burdensome stone for all people: all that burden themselves with it shall be cut in pieces, though all the people of the earth be gathered together against it."*

The <u>POWER</u> of God
will be displayed!

Isaiah 13:9-13 — *"Behold, the day of the LORD cometh, cruel both with wrath and fierce anger, to lay the land desolate: and He shall destroy the sinners thereof out of it. For the stars of heaven and the constellations thereof shall not give their light: the sun shall be darkened in his going forth, and the moon shall not cause her light to shine. And I will punish the world for their evil, and the wicked for their iniquity; and I will cause the arrogancy of the proud to cease, and will lay low the haughtiness of the terrible. I will make a man more precious than fine gold, even a man than the golden wedge of Ophir. Therefore I will shake the heavens, and the earth shall*

*remove out of her place, in the wrath of the LORD of hosts,
and in the day of His fierce anger."*

The <u>PEOPLE</u> of Israel will be delivered!

Ezekiel 37:25-28 — *"And they shall dwell in the land
that I have given unto Jacob My servant, wherein your fathers
have dwelt; and they shall dwell therein, even they, and their
children and their children's children forever: and My servant
David shall be their prince forever. Moreover I will make a
covenant of peace with them; it shall be an everlasting covenant with them: and I will place them, and multiply them,
and will set My sanctuary in the midst of them for evermore.
My tabernacle also shall be with them: yea, I will be their God,
and they shall be My people. And the heathen* (nations) *shall
know that I the LORD do sanctify Israel, when My sanctuary shall be in the midst of them forever more."*

Joel 2:32 — *"And it shall come to pass, that whosoever
shall call on the Name of the LORD shall be delivered: for
in mount Zion and in Jerusalem shall be deliverance, as the
LORD hath said, and in the remnant whom the LORD
shall call."*

Zechariah 12:10 — *"And I will pour upon the house
of David, and upon the inhabitants of Jerusalem, the Spirit
of grace and of supplications: and they shall look upon Me
Whom they have pierced, and they shall mourn for Him, as*

one mourneth for his only son, and shall be in bitterness for Him, as one that is in bitterness for his firstborn."

Zechariah 13:1 — *"In that day there shall be a fountain opened to the house of David and to the inhabitants of Jerusalem for sin and for uncleanness."*

Deliverance and salvation is coming for the people of Israel!

The <u>PROMISES</u> of God will be fulfilled!

Isaiah 46:9-11 — *"Remember the former things of old: for I am God, and there is none else; I am God, and there is none like Me, declaring the end from the beginning, and from ancient times the things that are not yet done, saying, My counsel shall stand, and I will do all My pleasure. Calling a ravenous bird from the east, the man that executeth My counsel from a far country; yea, I have spoken it, I will also bring it to pass; I have purposed it, I will also do it."*

Isaiah 55:10-11 — *"For as the rain cometh down, and the snow from heaven, and returneth not thither, but watereth the earth, and maketh it bring forth and bud, that it may give seed to the sower, and bread to the eater; So shall My word be that goeth forth out of My mouth: it shall not return unto me void, but it shall accomplish that which I please, and it shall prosper in the thing whereto I send it."*

Matthew 24:35 — *"Heaven and earth shall pass away, but My words shall not pass away."*

The promises of God will be fulfilled!

Everything that God said will happen in the future — will happen exactly as He said!

Chapter 27
THE MESSIANIC HOPE

Daniel the prophet made some incredible statements about the Messiah of Israel and the establishment of His kingdom on earth.

Daniel 2:44 — *"And in the days of these kings shall the God of Heaven set up a kingdom, which shall never be destroyed; and the kingdom shall not be left to other people, but it shall break in pieces and consume all these kingdoms, and it shall stand for ever."*

Daniel 7:13-14 — *"I saw in the night visions, and, behold, one like the Son of man came with the clouds of heaven, and came to the Ancient of Days, and they brought him near before Him. And there was given Him dominion, and glory, and a kingdom, that all people, nations, and languages, should serve Him: His dominion is an everlasting dominion which shall not pass away, and His kingdom that which shall not be destroyed."*

Isaiah the prophet said similar things:

Isaiah 9:6-7 — *"For unto us a child is born, unto us a son is given: and the government shall be upon His shoulder: and His Name shall be called Wonderful, Counsellor, The mighty God, The everlasting Father, The Prince of peace. Of the increase of His government and peace there shall be no end, upon the throne of David, and upon His kingdom, to order it, and to establish it with judgment and with justice from henceforth even forever. The zeal of the LORD of hosts will perform this."*

It is an everlasting kingdom — it will never be destroyed. The management of it will be *"on His shoulder"* alone!

Here are a few facts about this coming Messianic kingdom:

The Coming of the Messiah Will Make it All Possible!

Zechariah 14:9 — *"And the LORD shall be king over all the earth: in that day shall there be one LORD, and His Name one."*

Revelation 11:15 — *"The kingdoms of this world have become the kingdoms of our Lord, and of His Christ; and He shall reign forever and ever."*

Revelation 19:16 — *"And He hath on His vesture and on His thigh a Name written, KING of kings, and LORD of lords."*

The Conquest of All Nations Will be Achieved!

Isaiah 60:1-5 — *"Arise, shine; for thy light is come, and the glory of the LORD is risen upon thee. For, behold, the darkness shall cover the earth, and gross darkness the people: but the LORD shall arise upon thee, and His glory shall be seen upon thee. And the Gentiles* (nations) *shall come to Thy light, and kings to the brightness of Thy rising. Lift up thine eyes round about, and see: all they gather themselves together, they come to Thee: Thy sons shall come from far, and Thy daughters shall be nursed at Thy side. Then thou shalt see, and flow together, and thine heart shall fear, and be enlarged; because the abundance of the sea shall be converted unto Thee, the forces of the Gentiles shall come unto Thee."*

Revelation 19:15 — *"And out of His mouth goeth a sharp sword, that with it He should smite the nations: and He shall rule them with a rod of iron: and He treadeth the winepress of the fierceness and wrath of Almighty God."*

The Messiah will conquer all nations and they will submit to His leadership and authority!

The Conversion of Israel Will Come Before the Millennial Age Begins!

Isaiah 62:11 — *"Behold, the LORD hath proclaimed unto the end of the world, Say ye to the daughter of Zion,*

Behold, thy salvation cometh; behold, His reward is with Him, and His work before Him."

Micah 7:18-20 — "Who is a God like unto Thee, that pardoneth iniquity, and passeth by the transgression of the remnant of His heritage? He retaineth not His anger forever, because He delighteth in mercy. He will turn again, He will have compassion upon us; He will subdue our iniquities; and Thou wilt cast all their sins into the depths of the sea. Thou wilt perform the truth to Jacob, and the mercy to Abraham, which Thou hast sworn unto our fathers from the days of old."

Zechariah 12:10 — "And I will pour upon the house of David, and upon the inhabitants of Jerusalem, the Spirit of grace and of supplications: and they shall look upon Me Whom they have pierced, and they shall mourn for Him, as one mourneth for his only son, and shall be in bitterness for Him, as one that is in bitterness for his firstborn."

Romans 11:26 — "And so all Israel shall be saved: as it is written, There shall come out of Zion the Deliverer, and shall turn away ungodliness from Jacob."

The salvation of Israel does not include every person who is a Jew or lives in Israel. Zechariah 13:8-9 indicates that only one-third of the Nation will turn to the Messiah at the end of the Tribulation.

The Control of Satan Will Continue Throughout the Millennium!

Revelation 20:1-3 — *"And I saw an angel come down from heaven, having the key of the bottomless pit* (the abyss) *and a great chain in his hand. And he laid hold on the dragon, that old serpent, which is the Devil, and Satan, and bound him a thousand years, and cast him into the bottomless pit, and shut him up, and set a seal upon him, that he should deceive the nations no more, till the thousand years should be fulfilled: and after that he must be loosed a little season."*

The Confinement of Satan to the Lake of Fire Will Come at the End of the Millennial Reign of our Lord!

Revelation 20:7-10 — *"And when the thousand years are expired, Satan shall be loosed out of his prison, and shall go out to deceive the nations which are in the four quarters of the earth, Gog and Magog, to gather them together to battle: the number of whom is as the sand of the sea. And they went up on the breadth of the earth, and compassed the camp of the saints about, and the beloved city: and fire came down from God out of heaven, and devoured them. And the devil that deceived them was cast into the lake of fire and brimstone, where the beast and the false prophet are, and shall be tormented day and night forever and ever."*

Satan is NOT the king of hell — he is the chief prisoner!

The Construction of the Temple Will be Accomplished by the Messiah!

Isaiah 2:2-5 — *"And it shall come to pass in the last days, that the mountain of the LORD's house shall be established in the top of the mountains, and shall be exalted above the hills; and all nations shall flow unto it. And many people shall go and say, Come ye, and let us go up to the mountain of the LORD, to the house of the God of Jacob; and He will teach us His ways, and we will walk in His paths; for out of Zion shall go forth the law, and the word of the LORD from Jerusalem. And He shall judge among the nations, and shall rebuke many people: and they shall beat their swords into plowshares, and their spears into pruning hooks: nation shall not lift up sword against nation, neither shall they learn war any more. O house of Jacob, come ye, and let us walk in the light of the LORD."*

Amos 9:11 — *"In that day will I raise up the tabernacle of David that is fallen and close up the breaches thereof; and I will raise up his ruins, and I will built it as in the days of old."*

Zechariah 6:12-13 — *"Behold the Man Whose Name is The Branch; and He shall grow up out of His place, and He shall build the temple of the LORD. Even He shall build the temple of the LORD; and He shall bear the glory, and shall sit*

and rule upon His throne; and He shall be a priest upon His throne: and the counsel of peace shall be between them both."

The Messiah will build the Temple and shall be both King and Priest for His people. He will *"rule upon His throne"* — the throne of His father David — forever! May that blessed day come soon!

The Center of World Government Will be in Jerusalem!

Psalm 48:1-2 — *"Great is the LORD, and greatly to be praised in the city of our God, in the mountain of His holiness. Beautiful for situation, the joy of the whole earth, is mount Zion, on the sides of the north, the city of the great King."*

Psalm 48:8 — *"As we have heard, so have we seen in the city of the LORD of hosts, in the city of our God: God will establish it forever."*

Isaiah 65:17-25 — *"For, behold, I create new heavens and a new earth: and the former shall not be remembered, nor come into mind. But be ye glad and rejoice forever in that which I create: for, behold, I create Jerusalem a rejoicing, and her people a joy. And I will rejoice in Jerusalem, and joy in My people: and the voice of weeping shall be no more heard in her, nor the voice of crying. There shall be no more thence an infant of days, nor an old man that hath not filled his days: for the child shall die an hundred years old; but the sinner being an hundred years*

old shall be accursed. And they shall build houses, and inhabit them, and they shall plant vineyards, and eat the fruit of them. They shall not build, and another inhabit; they shall not plant, and another eat: for as the days of a tree are the days of My people, and Mine elect shall long enjoy the work of their hands. They shall not labor in vain, nor bring forth for trouble; for they are the seed of the blessed of the LORD, and their offspring with them. And it shall come to pass, that before they call, I will answer; and while they are yet speaking, I will hear. The wolf and the lamb shall feed together, and the lion shall eat straw like the bullock: and dust shall be the serpent's meat. They shall not hurt nor destroy in all My holy mountain, saith the LORD."

Zephaniah 3:16-17 — "In that day it shall be said to Jerusalem, Fear thou not: and to Zion, Let not thine hands be slack. The LORD thy God in the midst of thee is mighty; He will save, He will rejoice over thee with joy; He will rest in His love, He will joy over thee with singing."

The Messiah's throne will be in Jerusalem, and from that future city the word of the Lord will go forth to the whole world. All nations will come to Jerusalem to worship the Lord!

The Condition for Entering the Messianic Kingdom is Very Clear!

Matthew 18:4 — "Verily I say unto you, Except ye be

converted, and become as little children, ye shall not enter the kingdom of heaven."

John 3:3-5 — *"Jesus answered and said unto him (Nicodemus), Verily, verily, I say unto thee, Except a man be born again, he cannot see the kingdom of God. Nicodemus saith unto Him, How can a man be born when he is old? Can he enter the second time into his mother's womb, and be born? Jesus answered, Verily, verily, I say unto thee, Except a man be born of water and of the Spirit, he cannot enter into the kingdom of God."*

I Corinthians 6:9-11 — *"Know ye not that the unrighteous shall not inherit the kingdom of God? Be not deceived: neither fornicators, nor idolaters, nor adulterers, nor effeminate, nor abusers of themselves with mankind, nor thieves, nor covetous, nor drunkards, nor revilers, nor extortioners, shall inherit the kingdom of God. And such were some of you: but ye are washed, but ye are sanctified, but ye are justified in the Name of the Lord Jesus, and by the Spirit of our God."*

Galatians 5:19-21 — *"Now the works of the flesh are manifest, which are these; Adultery, fornication, uncleanness, lasciviousness, idolatry, witchcraft, hatred, variance, emulations, wrath, strife, seditions, heresies, envyings, murders, drunkenness, revellings, and such like: of the which I tell you before, as I have also told you in time past, that they which do such things shall not inherit the kingdom of God."*

Today's culture believes that even if you do the things listed above, God will let you into heaven if your good deeds are greater than your evil deeds! Such false teaching has deceived many so-called "Christians." We are not genuine Christians on the basis of what we do or don't do — it is faith in the <u>finished work of the Messiah</u> that brings salvation and entrance into the kingdom of God!

Ephesians 5:5 — *"For this ye know, that no whoremonger, nor unclean person, nor covetous man, who is an idolater, hath any inheritance in the kingdom of Christ and of God."*

Colossians 1:13-14 — *"Who hath delivered us from the power of darkness, and hath translated us into the kingdom of His dear Son: In Whom we have redemption through His blood, even the forgiveness of sins."*

II Timothy 4:18 — *"And the Lord shall deliver me from every evil work, and will preserve me unto His heavenly kingdom: to Whom be glory forever and ever. Amen!"*

II Peter 1:11 — *"For so an entrance shall be ministered unto you abundantly into the everlasting kingdom of our Lord and Savior Jesus Christ."*

Is Faith in the Messiah of Israel an Essential for Getting into the Messianic Kingdom?

Our answer is a firm "YES!" The Bible makes it very clear. In the Jewish Bible in Isaiah 45:22 the Messiah says:

"Look unto Me, and be ye saved, all the ends of the earth: for I am God, and there is none else."

In the New Testament, in John 20:30-31 we read:

"And many other signs truly did Jesus in the presence of His disciples, which are not written in this book; But these are written, that ye might believe that Jesus (Yeshua) is the Christ (Messiah), the Son of God; and that believing ye might have life through His Name."

The Jewish Targum, Midrash, and Talmud speak of the Messiah in 62 separate verses in the book of Isaiah alone!

Isaiah 9:1-2 speaks of the *"light"* that shines upon the *"nations"* who walk in the darkness — passages that are quoted in the NT (*Matthew 4:13-16*) as referring to Yeshua — the rabbinical writings of the past, before His time, speak of this *"light"* as being the Messiah Himself!

Yeshua said in John 8:12: *"I am the light of the world; he that followeth Me shall not walk in darkness, but have the light of life."*

One of the most powerful passages about the Messiah of Israel is found in Isaiah 9:6-7:

"For unto us a child is born, unto us a son is given: and the government shall be upon His shoulder: and His Name shall be called Wonderful, Counsellor, The Mighty God, The everlasting Father, The Prince of peace. Of the increase of His government and peace there shall be no end,

upon the throne of David, and upon His kingdom, to order it, and to establish it with judgment and with justice from henceforth even forever. The zeal of the LORD of hosts will perform this."

Consider the following issues as they relate to the true identity of the Messiah and our assurance of entering the Messianic kingdom:

His Presence Will Identify Him With Humanity

"For unto us a child is born, unto us a son is given" — The word *"for"* connects the context by teaching that there is great rejoicing among God's people, because God has broken the yoke of oppression, and the weapons and garments of the warrior are destroyed, and the basic reason for these blessings is that a special *"child"* is born. In contrast to Assyria and the Syrian/northern Israel coalition, a *"child"* will bring deliverance to God's people!

In the TARGUM OF ISAIAH we read of this verse: *"and there was called His name from of old, Wonderful Counselor, Mighty God, He who lives forever, the Messiah, in whose days peace shall increase upon us."*

His Position Will Identify Him With Sovereignty

"and the government shall be upon His shoulder" — In Isaiah 22:22 we read: *"the key of the house of David will I lay upon his shoulder; so he shall open and none shall shut; and he shall shut, and none shall open. And I will fasten him as a nail in a sure place; and he shall be for a glorious throne to his father's house."*

His Person Will Identify Him With Deity!

"and His name shall be called…" — The word *"name"* refers not to a title by which He will be addressed, but rather His nature, attributes, and abilities.

- ✦ He is <u>INCOMPREHENSIBLE</u>! — *"wonderful counselor"*

- ✦ He is <u>INVINCIBLE</u>! — *"the mighty God"* (Hebrew: *El Gibbor*)

- ✦ He is <u>INCORRUPTIBLE</u>! — *"the everlasting Father."* The Hebrew word — *'ad* — implies duration or that which is unending. The phrase may be rendered in two ways: *"the Father of eternity"* or *"one who is eternally a Father."*

- ✦ He is <u>INCOMPARABLE</u>! — *"the Prince of peace."*

His Peace Will Identify Him With Royalty!

"of the increase of His government and peace there shall be no end, upon the throne of David, and upon His kingdom, to order it, and to establish it with judgment and with justice from henceforth even forever"

His Power Will Identify Him With Majesty!

"The zeal of the LORD of hosts will perform this"— In Isaiah 45:23 we read: *"I have sworn by Myself, the word is gone out of My mouth in righteousness, and shall not turn, That unto Me every knee shall bow, every tongue shall swear."*

In the New Testament, in Philippians 2:9-11 it quotes the above passage from Isaiah:

"Wherefore God also hath highly exalted Him, and given Him a Name which is above every name: That at the Name of Jesus every knee should bow, of things in heaven, and things in earth, and things under the earth; And that every tongue should confess that Jesus Christ is Lord, to the glory of God the Father."

Have you personally confessed Jesus Christ as your Lord and Savior? Do you believe that He died for your sins, was buried, and rose again to bring eternal life to all who will believe?

The Messiah of Israel is the only hope of Israel and you and me!

To God be all the Glory!